TERRORISM

OPPOSING VIEWPOINTS®

OTHER BOOKS OF RELATED INTEREST

OPPOSING VIEWPOINTS SERIES
Africa
American Foreign Policy
The Breakup of the Soviet Union
Central America
Eastern Europe
Islam
The Middle East
The New World Order
The Third World
War
Weapons of Mass Destruction

CURRENT CONTROVERSIES SERIES
Europe
Hunger
Interventionism
Iraq
Nationalism and Ethnic Conflict

AT ISSUE SERIES
Ethnic Conflict
The United Nations
U.S. Policy Toward China

TERRORISM

OPPOSING VIEWPOINTS®

Laura K. Egendorf, Book Editor

David L. Bender, Publisher

Bruno Leone, Executive Editor

Bonnie Szumski, Editorial Director

David M. Haugen, Managing Editor

OPPOSING
VIEWPOINTS®
SERIES

Greenhaven Press, Inc., San Diego, California

Cover photo: PhotoDisc

Library of Congress Cataloging-in-Publication Data

Terrorism : opposing viewpoints / Laura K. Egendorf, book editor.
       p.   cm. — (Opposing viewpoints series)
     Includes bibliographical references and index.
     ISBN 0-7377-0137-4 (alk. paper). —
   ISBN 0-7377-0136-6 (pbk. : alk. paper)
     1. Terrorism. 2. Political violence. I. Egendorf, Laura K., 1973–   .
   II. Series: Opposing viewpoints series (Unnumbered)
   HV6431.T485 2000
   363.3'2—dc21
                                                        99-10356
                                                          CIP

Greenhaven Press, Inc., P.O. Box 289009
San Diego, CA 92198-9009

"CONGRESS SHALL MAKE NO LAW. . . ABRIDGING THE FREEDOM OF SPEECH, OR OF THE PRESS."

First Amendment to the U.S. Constitution

The basic foundation of our democracy is the First Amendment guarantee of freedom of expression. The Opposing Viewpoints Series is dedicated to the concept of this basic freedom and the idea that it is more important to practice it than to enshrine it.

CONTENTS

WHY CONSIDER
OPPOSING VIEWPOINTS?

"The only way in which a human being can make some approach to knowing the whole of a subject is by hearing what can be said about it by persons of every variety of opinion and studying all modes in which it can be looked at by every character of mind. No wise man ever acquired his wisdom in any mode but this."

John Stuart Mill

In our media-intensive culture it is not difficult to find differing opinions. Thousands of newspapers and magazines and dozens of radio and television talk shows resound with differing points of view. The difficulty lies in deciding which opinion to agree with and which "experts" seem the most credible. The more inundated we become with differing opinions and claims, the more essential it is to hone critical reading and thinking skills to evaluate these ideas. Opposing Viewpoints books address this problem directly by presenting stimulating debates that can be used to enhance and teach these skills. The varied opinions contained in each book examine many different aspects of a single issue. While examining these conveniently edited opposing views, readers can develop critical thinking skills such as the ability to compare and contrast authors' credibility, facts, argumentation styles, use of persuasive techniques, and other stylistic tools. In short, the Opposing Viewpoints Series is an ideal way to attain the higher-level thinking and reading skills so essential in a culture of diverse and contradictory opinions.

In addition to providing a tool for critical thinking, Opposing Viewpoints books challenge readers to question their own strongly held opinions and assumptions. Most people form their opinions on the basis of upbringing, peer pressure, and personal, cultural, or professional bias. By reading carefully balanced opposing views, readers must directly confront new ideas as well as the opinions of those with whom they disagree. This is not to simplistically argue that everyone who reads opposing views will—or should—change his or her opinion. Instead, the series enhances readers' understanding of their own views by encouraging confrontation with opposing ideas. Careful examination of others' views can lead to the readers' understanding of the logical inconsistencies in their own opinions, perspective on why they hold an opinion, and the consideration of the possibility that their opinion requires further evaluation.

EVALUATING OTHER OPINIONS

To ensure that this type of examination occurs, Opposing Viewpoints books present all types of opinions. Prominent spokespeople on different sides of each issue as well as well-known professionals from many disciplines challenge the reader. An additional goal of the series is to provide a forum for other, less known, or even unpopular viewpoints. The opinion of an ordinary person who has had to make the decision to cut off life support from a terminally ill relative, for example, may be just as valuable and provide just as much insight as a medical ethicist's professional opinion. The editors have two additional purposes in including these less known views. One, the editors encourage readers to respect others' opinions—even when not enhanced by professional credibility. It is only by reading or listening to and objectively evaluating others' ideas that one can determine whether they are worthy of consideration. Two, the inclusion of such viewpoints encourages the important critical thinking skill of objectively evaluating an author's credentials and bias. This evaluation will illuminate an author's reasons for taking a particular stance on an issue and will aid in readers' evaluation of the author's ideas.

As series editors of the Opposing Viewpoints Series, it is our hope that these books will give readers a deeper understanding of the issues debated and an appreciation of the complexity of even seemingly simple issues when good and honest people disagree. This awareness is particularly important in a democratic society such as ours in which people enter into public debate to determine the common good. Those with whom one disagrees should not be regarded as enemies but rather as people whose views deserve careful examination and may shed light on one's own.

Thomas Jefferson once said that "difference of opinion leads to inquiry, and inquiry to truth." Jefferson, a broadly educated man, argued that "if a nation expects to be ignorant and free . . . it expects what never was and never will be." As individuals and as a nation, it is imperative that we consider the opinions of others and examine them with skill and discernment. The Opposing Viewpoints Series is intended to help readers achieve this goal.

David L. Bender & Bruno Leone,
Series Editors

Greenhaven Press anthologies primarily consist of previously published material taken from a variety of sources, including periodicals, books, scholarly journals, newspapers, government documents, and position papers from private and public organizations. These original sources are often edited for length and to ensure their accessibility for a young adult audience. The anthology editors also change the original titles of these works in order to clearly present the main thesis of each viewpoint and to explicitly indicate the opinion presented in the viewpoint. These alterations are made in consideration of both the reading and comprehension levels of a young adult audience. Every effort is made to ensure that Greenhaven Press accurately reflects the original intent of the authors included in this anthology.

INTRODUCTION

"Small groups of terrorists can do tremendous damage. . . .
That is really the essence of terrorism—to intimidate and
influence a far wider audience."
—Philip Wilcox, former coordinator of counterterrorism for the U.S.
State Department

"Terrorism is what 'others' do. 'We' do not practice terrorism."
—Edna Homa Hunt, writer for Washington
Report on Middle East Affairs

"One man's terrorist is another man's freedom fighter." As that
adage suggests, it is nearly impossible to provide a universal definition of terrorism. Efforts to define terrorism are influenced by
one's perspective. While there may be no one-size-fits-all definition, certain interpretations have garnered particular attention.

The Western perspective on terrorism, particularly that of the
United States, offers a useful starting point. The U.S. State Department and the Federal Bureau of Investigation (FBI) play key
roles in the fight against international and domestic terrorism
and provide what can be considered as the official U.S. definitions. According to the State Department, terrorism is "premedi-
tated, politically motivated violence perpetrated against non-
combatant targets by subnational groups or clandestine agents
usually intended to influence an audience." The FBI states that
terrorism "is the unlawful use of force or violence against persons or property . . . in furtherance of political or social objectives." According to the State Department's terminology, active
terrorist groups include Japan's Aum Shinrikyo, the Palestinian
territories' Hamas, Lebanon's Hezbollah, Israel's Kahane Chai,
and Peru's Shining Path. The FBI definition broadens the scope
to include domestic terrorist groups in its rubric, such as extremist militia organizations that might pose a threat to the U.S.
government. Regardless of the definition, all of these organizations are considered to have the same objective—the intimida-
tion, usually by violent means, of others in order to achieve the
groups' political goals.

While the U.S. government might be satisfied with these definitions, those who it labels terrorists—and those who might
support the groups' views—are not. For example, while the FBI
might consider a militia organization to be a terrorist threat, the

members of that organization are likely to see themselves as defenders of American values that they believe have been demolished by a corrupt U.S. government. Likewise, Saudi Arabian millionaire Osama Bin Ladin, viewed by the United States as a terrorist mastermind, has argued that he is not a terrorist, but rather someone fighting a holy war against America. According to Bin Ladin, he is fighting America because he believes the United States has behaved cruelly toward Arabs through actions such as supporting Israel and imposing sanctions upon Iraq—sanctions that have reportedly led to the deaths of one million Iraqi children. Terrorists—whether they are opposing their own country's government or that of another nation—behave the way that they do because they do not consider less-violent methods (such as diplomacy or peaceful protests) to be viable options.

It is not only the purported terrorists who disagree with the way they have been characterized. Other people, who may disagree with American policies or empathize with the views of these alleged terrorists (while not being terrorists themselves), assert that the U.S. definition of terrorism is politically motivated. Those organizations whose political views run counter to American policy are unfairly labeled terrorists, these critics argue. In an article in the People's Weekly World, reporter Emile Schepers writes, "It is quite certain that the criteria [for the State Department list] was not based on a genuine law enforcement interest in combating terrorism but, rather, almost entirely on U.S. international strategic considerations." For example, Schepers notes, right-wing organizations in Latin America that have bombed hotels and formed death squads are excluded from the list, while left-wing groups in the region that have no connection to international terrorism are deemed dangerous. Some analysts note that the State Department list also selectively excludes certain groups that may use terrorist tactics. The Irish Republican Army (IRA), for example, is among the excluded organizations, Schepers argues, because the United States wants to play a key role in the Northern Ireland peace process. The State Department has asserted that the IRA was not included on the October 1997 list (though it had been listed in previous years) because the group declared a ceasefire in July 1997.

Not only do many people disagree with the American definition of terrorism, but some even argue that one name is missing from the State Department list—the United States itself. For example, many people viewed the Clinton administration's decision in August 1998 to bomb chemical factories and alleged terrorist camps in Sudan and Afghanistan, in response to the bombings of U.S. embassies in Kenya and Tanzania, as a terrorist response to terrorism. Columnist Norman Solomon argues that the U.S. actions are based on Orwellian ideas. He writes: "When terrorists attack, they're terrorizing. When we attack, we're retaliating." Within the United States, militia groups have often argued that it is the U.S. government that is the real danger, labeling the fiery end of the Branch Davidian standoff in Waco, Texas, a terrorist act on the part of the FBI and Bureau of Alcohol, Tobacco, and Firearms (BATF). Other observers assert that the United States has promoted terrorism in Central America, the Middle East, and elsewhere.

Understandably, the U.S. government, along with some supporters, disputes this point of view. At a U.S. State Department press briefing on August 21, 1998, Under Secretary of State Thomas Pickering defended the Sudan and Afghanistan bombings. "Our strikes against terrorist targets in Afghanistan and Sudan . . . represent an intensification in our battle against terror. . . . The main purpose of the strikes was to prevent further terrorist attacks against American targets, not a retaliation." Politicians from both major political parties and editorials in numerous publications also supported the United States' actions, with some people suggesting that the nation needs to use even more force to quell terrorism. Mortimer B. Zuckerman, the editor-in-chief of U.S. News & World Report, asserted, "The United States must lead the world in an unrelenting campaign against terrorist groups and the states that harbor them."

The disputes, throughout the United States and the rest of the world, over America's foreign and domestic policies help explain why a universal definition of terrorism may never be formulated. Nonetheless, while the world may not be able to agree on what terrorism is, its impact on modern society cannot be ignored. Terrorism: Opposing Viewpoints considers terrorism's place in today's world in the following chapters: Is Terrorism a Serious Threat? What Motivates Terrorists? Can Terrorism Be Justified? How Should the United States Respond to Terrorism? In these chapters, the authors debate the extent of and reasons for terrorism and ways the threat can be lessened.

Is Terrorism a Serious Threat?

CHAPTER PREFACE

When a major terrorist attack, such as the Oklahoma City bombing, occurs, the newspapers and magazines during the next several weeks are filled with stories about the event. Ideally, media coverage provides an accurate indication of the threat and extent of terrorism. However, many people argue that the media are not always objective reporters. Instead, they contend the media often overstate the threat of terrorism and at times can even increase the danger.

Some analysts argue that the relationship between the media—especially television—and terrorism is a two-way street. The visuals shown on television, of destroyed buildings and grieving survivors, present a dynamic way for terrorists to disseminate their views. Joseph Eliot Magnet, a law professor at Ottawa University in Canada, observes, "Through a theatrical display of horror and spectacle, terrorism enables a weak political message . . . to exert a strong psychological impact upon a vast audience." Reporting on acts of terror allow the media to grab larger audiences. Ehud Sprinzak, a professor of political science at Hebrew University in Jerusalem, writes, "[Even] as media outlets spin the new frenzy [the fear of superterrorism] out of personal and financial interests, they also respond to the deep psychological needs of a huge audience. People love to be horrified." These observers and others argue that the media allow terrorists to appear as greater threats than they truly are. In addition, some people maintain, the media overstate the terrorist threat posed by certain groups, such as Muslims and militia members.

Other writers argue that the overblown coverage becomes a self-fulfilling prophecy, because some terrorists might seek further notoriety by instigating additional attacks. David Rapoport, the joint editor of *Terrorism and Political Violence*, writes that publicity can help terrorist groups attract new followers and sympathizers. Alex P. Schmid, the author and editor of several books on terrorism, has argued that media coverage of terrorism might lead to copycat attacks. In these instances, the observers claim, the media fail in their role to merely report the news. Rather, the media outlets become instigators in the process and create threats that perhaps did not exist before.

Much controversy persists over whether terrorism poses a serious threat. The authors in this chapter consider whether the possibility of terrorism has increased or if the risks have been unduly magnified.

VIEWPOINT

"Terrorism today has arguably
become more complex, amorphous
and transnational."

TERRORISM IS A SERIOUS THREAT

Bruce Hoffman

In the following viewpoint, Bruce Hoffman argues that while the number of terrorist incidents has declined in the 1990s, the incidents have become deadlier. He asserts that the factors leading to the increase in fatalities include the rise in religious terrorism and the proliferation of amateur terrorists. According to Hoffman, terrorists are also more likely to rely on violence as an end in itself and less inclined to justify their actions and reasoning. Hoffman is the director of the Centre for the Study of Terrorism at St. Andrews University in Scotland. This viewpoint was originally a paper presented at the International Conference on Aviation Safety and Security in the 21st Century, held January 13–15, 1997.

As you read, consider the following questions:

1. According to statistics cited by Hoffman, what percentage of terrorist incidents in 1995 resulted in at least one fatality?
2. In the author's view, how have terrorist methods become more accessible to amateurs?
3. The Tokyo subway nerve gas attack typifies which worrisome trend in terrorism, according to Hoffman?

Excerpted from Bruce Hoffman, "The Confluence of International and Domestic Trends in Terrorism," *Terrorism and Political Violence*, Summer 1997. Reprinted by permission of Frank Cass, publishers.

A lthough the total volume of terrorist incidents world-wide has declined in the 1990s, the proportion of people killed in terrorist incidents has steadily risen. For example, according to the RAND-St Andrews University Chronology of International Terrorism, a record 484 international terrorist incidents were recorded in 1991, the year of the Gulf War, followed by 343 incidents in 1992, 360 in 1993, 353 in 1994, and falling to 278 incidents in 1995 (the last calendar year for which complete statistics are available). However, while international terrorists were becoming less active, they were nonetheless becoming more lethal. For example, at least one person was killed in 29 per cent of terrorist incidents in 1995: the highest percentage of fatalities to incidents recorded in the Chronology since 1968—and an increase of two per cent over the previous year's record figure. In the United States this trend was most clearly reflected in the 1995 bombing of the Alfred P. Murrah Federal Building in Oklahoma City. Since the turn of the century, fewer than a dozen of all the terrorist incidents committed world-wide have killed more than a 100 people. The 168 people confirmed dead at the Murrah Building ranks sixth on the list of most fatalities caused this century in a single terrorist incident—domestic or international.

The reasons for terrorism's increasing lethality are complex and variegated, but can generally be summed up as follows:

- The growth in the number of terrorist groups motivated by a religious imperative;
- The proliferation of 'amateurs' involved in terrorist acts; and
- The increasing sophistication and operational competence of 'professional' terrorists.

RELIGIOUS TERRORISM HAS INCREASED

The increase of terrorism motivated by a religious imperative neatly encapsulates the confluence of new adversaries, motivations and rationales affecting terrorist patterns today. Admittedly, the connection between religion and terrorism is not new. However, while religion and terrorism do share a long history, in recent decades this form of particular variant has largely been overshadowed by ethnic- and nationalist-separatist or ideologically-motivated terrorism. Indeed, none of the 11 identifiable terrorist groups active in 1968 (the year credited with marking the advent of modern, international terrorism) could be classified as 'religious'. Not until 1980 in fact—as a result of the repercussions from the revolution in Iran the year before—do the first 'modern' religious terrorist groups appear: but they amount to only two of the 64 groups active that year. Twelve years later, however, the number of religious terrorist groups has increased nearly six-fold, representing a quarter (11 of 48) of the terrorist organisations who carried out attacks in 1992. Significantly, this trend has not only continued, but has actually accelerated. By 1994, a third (16) of the 49 identifiable terrorist groups could be classified as religious in character and/or motivation. In 1995, their number increased yet again, now to account for nearly half (25 or 45 per cent) of the 58 known terrorist groups [that were] active.

The implications of terrorism motivated by a religious imperative for higher levels of lethality is evidenced by the violent record of various Shi'a Islamic groups during the 1980s. For example, although these organisations committed only eight per cent of all recorded international terrorist incidents between 1982 and 1989, they were nonetheless responsible for nearly 30 per cent of the total number of deaths during that time period. Indeed, some of the most significant terrorist acts of the past 18 months, for example, have all had some religious element present. Even more disturbing is that in some instances the perpetrators' aims have gone beyond the establishment of some theocracy amenable to their specific deity, but have embraced mystical, almost transcendental, and divinely-inspired imperatives or a vehemently anti-government form of 'populism' reflecting far-fetched conspiracy notions based on a volatile mixture of seditious, racial and religious dicta.

Religious terrorism tends to be more lethal than secular terrorism because of the radically different value systems, mechanisms of legitimisation and justification, concepts of morality and Manichaean world views that directly affect the 'holy terrorists' motivation. For the religious terrorist, violence first and foremost is a sacramental act or divine duty: executed in direct response to some theological demand or imperative and justified by scripture. Religion, therefore, functions as a legitimising force: specifically sanctioning wide-scale violence against an almost open-ended category of opponents (e.g., all peoples who are not members of the religious terrorists' religion or cult). This explains why clerical sanction is so important for religious terrorists and why religious figures are often required to 'bless' (e.g., approve) terrorist operations before they are executed.

THE THREAT OF AMATEUR TERRORISM

The proliferation of 'amateurs' involved in terrorist acts has also contributed to terrorism's increasing lethality. In the past, terrorism was not just a matter of having the will and motivation to act, but of having the capability to do so—the requisite training, access to weaponry and operational knowledge. These were not readily available capabilities and were generally acquired through training undertaken in camps known to be run either by other terrorist organisations and/or in concert with the terrorists' state-sponsors. Today, however, the means and methods of terrorism can be easily obtained at bookstores, from mail-order publishers, on CD-ROM or even over the Internet. Hence, terrorism has become accessible to anyone with a grievance, an agenda, a purpose or any idiosyncratic combination of the above.

THE FUTURE OF TERRORISM

In the past, terrorism was almost always the province of groups of militants that had the backing of political forces like the Irish and Russian social revolutionary movements of 1900. In the future, terrorists will be individuals or like-minded people working in very small groups, on the pattern of the technology-hating Unabomber, who apparently worked alone sending out parcel bombs over two decades, or the perpetrators of the 1995 bombing of the federal building in Oklahoma City. An individual may possess the technical competence to steal, buy, or manufacture the weapons he or she needs for a terrorist purpose; he or she may or may not require help from one or two others in delivering these weapons to the designated target. The ideologies such individuals and mini-groups espouse are likely to be even more aberrant than those of larger groups. And terrorists working alone or in very small groups will be more difficult to detect unless they make a major mistake or are discovered by accident.

Walter Laquer, *Foreign Affairs*, September/October 1996.

Relying on these commercially obtainable published bomb-making manuals and operational guidebooks, the 'amateur' terrorist can be just as deadly and destructive—and even more difficult to track and anticipate—than his 'professional' counterpart. In this respect, the alleged 'Unabomber', Theodore Kaczynski, is a case in point. From a remote cabin in the Montana hinterland, Kaczynski is believed to have fashioned simple, yet sophisticated home-made bombs from ordinary materials that were dispatched to his victims via the post. Despite one of the most massive manhunts staged by the FBI in the United States, the 'Unabomber' was nonetheless able to elude capture—much less identification—for 18 years and indeed to kill three people and injure 23 others. Hence, the 'Unabomber' is an example of the difficulties confronting law enforcement and other government authorities in first identifying, much less apprehending the 'amateur' terrorist and the minimal skills needed to wage an effective terrorist campaign. This case also evidences the disproportionately extensive consequences even violence committed by a lone individual can have both on society (in terms of the fear and panic sown) and on law enforcement (because of the vast resources that are devoted to the identification and apprehension of this individual).

'Amateur' terrorists are dangerous in other ways as well. In fact, the absence of some central command authority may result in fewer constraints on the terrorists' operations and targets and—especially when combined with a religious fervour—fewer inhibitions on their desire to inflict indiscriminate casualties. Israeli authorities, for example, have noted this pattern among terrorists belonging to the radical Palestinian Islamic Hamas organisation in contrast to their predecessors in the ostensibly more secular and professional, centrally-controlled mainstream Palestine Liberation Organization terrorist groups. As one senior Israeli security official noted of a particularly vicious band of Hamas terrorists: they 'were a surprisingly unprofessional bunch . . . they had no preliminary training and acted without specific instructions'.

In the United States, to cite another example of the potentially destructive lethal power of amateur terrorists, it is suspected that the 1993 World Trade Center bombers' intent was in fact to bring down one of the twin towers. By contrast, there is no evidence that the people we once considered to be the world's arch-terrorists—the Carloses [Ilich Ramirez Sanchez, also known as Carlos the Jackal], Abu Nidals and Abul Abbases—ever contemplated, much less attempted, to destroy a high-rise office building packed with people. . . .

INCREASED SOPHISTICATION

Finally, while on the one hand terrorism is attracting 'amateurs', on the other hand the sophistication and operational competence of the 'professional' terrorists is also increasing. These 'professionals' are becoming demonstrably more adept in their trade craft of death and destruction; more formidable in their abilities of tactical modification, adjustment and innovation in their methods of attack; and appear to be able to operate for sustained periods of time while avoiding detection, interception and arrest or capture. More disquieting, these 'professional' terrorists are apparently becoming considerably more ruthless as well. An almost Darwinian principle of natural selection seems to affect subsequent generations of terrorist groups, whereby every new terrorist generation learns from its predecessors, becoming smarter, tougher and more difficult to capture or eliminate.

Accordingly, it is not difficult to recognise how the 'amateur' terrorist may become increasingly attractive to either a more professional terrorist group and/or their state patron as a pawn or 'cut-out' or simply as an expendable minion. In this manner, the 'amateur' terrorist could be effectively used by others to further conceal the identity of the foreign government or terrorist group actually commissioning or ordering a particular attack. . . .

DANGEROUS TRENDS

While it can be argued that the terrorist threat is declining in terms of the total number of annual incidents in other, perhaps more significant, respects—e.g., both the number of people killed in individual terrorist incidents and the percentage of terrorist incidents with fatalities in comparison to total incidents—the threat is actually rising. Accordingly, it is as important to look at qualitative changes as well as quantitative ones; and to focus on generic threat and generic capabilities based on overall trends as well as on known or existing groups.

The pitfalls of focusing on known, identifiable groups at the expense of other potential, less-easily identified, more amorphous adversaries was perhaps most clearly demonstrated in Japan by the attention long paid to familiar and well-established left-wing groups like the Japanese Red Army or Middle Core organisation with an established *modus operandi*, identifiable leadership, etc., rather than on an obscure, relatively unknown religious movement, such as the Aum Shinrikyo sect. Indeed, the Aum sect's nerve gas attack on the Tokyo underground demarcates a significant historical watershed in terrorist tactics and weaponry. This incident clearly demonstrated that it is possible—even for ostensibly 'amateur' terrorists—to execute a successful chemical terrorist attack and, accordingly, may conceivably have raised the stakes for terrorists everywhere. Terrorist groups in the future may well feel driven to emulate or surpass the Tokyo incident either in death and destruction or in the use of a non-conventional weapon of mass destruction (WMD) in order to ensure the same media coverage and public attention as the nerve gas attack generated.

The Tokyo incident also highlights another troubling trend in terrorism: significantly, groups today claim credit for attacks less frequently than in the past. They tend not to take responsibility, much less issue communiqués explaining why they carried out an attack as the stereotypical, 'traditional' terrorist group of the past did. . . .

The implication of this trend is perhaps that violence for some terrorist groups is becoming less a means to an end (that therefore has to be calibrated and tailored and therefore 'explained' and 'justified' to the public) than an end in itself that does not require any wider explanation or justification beyond the groups' members themselves and perhaps their specific followers. Such a trait would conform not only to the motivations of religious terrorists (discussed above) but also to terrorist 'spoilers'—groups bent on disrupting or sabotaging multilateral negotiations or the peaceful settlement of ethnic conflicts or other such violent disputes. That terrorists are less frequently claiming credit for their attacks may suggest an inevitable loosening of constraints—self-imposed or otherwise—on their violence: in turn leading to higher levels of lethality as well.

TERRORISM AND TECHNOLOGY

Another key factor contributing to the rising terrorist threat is the ease of terrorist adaptations across the technological spectrum. For example, on the low-end of the technological spectrum one sees terrorists continuing to rely on fertiliser bombs whose devastating effect has been demonstrated by the Provisional Irish Republican Army (PIRA) at St Mary Axe and Bishop's Gate in 1991 and 1992; at Canary Wharf and in Manchester in 1996; by the aforementioned World Trade Center bombers and the people responsible for the Oklahoma City bombing. . . .

On the high-end of the conflict spectrum one must contend not only with the efforts of groups like the Aum to develop chemical, biological and nuclear weapons capabilities, but with the proliferation of fissile materials from the former Soviet Union and the emergent illicit market in nuclear materials that is surfacing in eastern and central Europe. Admittedly, while much of the material seen on offer as part of this 'black market' cannot be classified as SNM (strategic nuclear material, that is suitable in the construction of a fissionable explosive device), such highly toxic radioactive agents can potentially be easily paired with conventional explosives and turned into a crude, non-fissionable atomic bomb (e.g., 'dirty' bomb). Such a device would therefore not only physically destroy a target, but contaminate the surrounding area for decades to come.

Finally, at the middle-end of the spectrum one sees a world awash in plastic explosives, hand-held precision-guided-munitions (i.e., surface-to-air missiles for use against civilian and/or military aircraft), automatic weapons, etc., that readily facilitate all types of terrorist operations. During the 1980s, Czechoslovakia, for example, sold 1,000 tonnes of Semtex-H (the explosive of which eight ounces was sufficient to bring down Pan Am 103) to Libya and another 40,000 tonnes to Syria, North Korea, Iran and Iraq—countries long cited by the US Department of State as sponsors of international terrorist activity. In sum, terrorists therefore have relatively easy access to a range of sophisticated, 'off-the-shelf' weapons technology that can be readily adapted to their operational needs.

THE BLURRING OF DOMESTIC AND INTERNATIONAL TERRORISM

Terrorism today has arguably become more complex, amorphous and transnational. The distinction between domestic and international terrorism is also evaporating as evidenced by the Aum sect's activities in Russia and Australia as well as in Japan, the alleged links between the Oklahoma City bombers and neo-Nazis in Britain and Europe, and the network of Algerian Islamic extremists operating in France, Great Britain, Sweden, Belgium and other countries as well as in Algeria itself. Accordingly, as these threats are both domestic and international, the response must therefore be both national as well as multinational in construct and dimensions. National cohesiveness and organisational preparation will necessarily remain the essential foundation for any hope of building the effective multinational approach appropriate to these new threats. Without internal (national or domestic) consistency, clarity, planning and organisation, it will be impossible for similarly diffuse multinational efforts to succeed. This is all the more critical today, and will remain so in the future, given the changing nature of the terrorist threat, the identity of its perpetrators and the resources at their disposal.

One final point is in order on the topic of aviation security. Serious and considerable though the above trends are, their implications for—much less direct effect on—commercial aviation are by no means clear. Despite media impressions to the contrary and the popular mis-perception fostered by those impressions, terrorist attacks on civil aviation—particularly inflight bombings or attempted bombings—are in fact relatively rare. Indeed, they account for only 15 of the 2,537 international terrorist incidents recorded between 1970 and 1979 (or .006 per cent) and just 12 of 3,943 recorded between 1980 and 1989 (an even lower .003 per cent). This trend, moreover, has continued throughout the first half of the current decade. . . .

Nonetheless, those charged with ensuring the security of airports and aviation from terrorist threats doubtless face a Herculean task. In the first place, a defence that would preclude every possible attack by every possible terrorist group for every possible motive is not even theoretically conceivable. Accordingly, security measures should accurately and closely reflect both the threat and the difficulties inherent in countering it: and should therefore be based on realistic expectations that embrace realistic cost-benefit. Indeed, there is a point beyond which security measures may not only be inappropriate to the presumed threat, but risk becoming more bureaucratic than genuinely effective.

"Public fears and government comments notwithstanding, terrorism is not on the rise."

THE THREAT OF TERRORISM IS OVERSTATED

Larry C. Johnson

The prevalence and lethality of terrorism is decreasing, maintains Larry C. Johnson in the following viewpoint. Johnson claims that, compared to terrorist acts from the 1980s, terrorism in the 1990s is less deadly and involves fewer groups and countries. He asserts that the decline in incidents and fatalities is due to tougher government policies, more powerful law enforcement, and the fall of communism. Johnson is a former employee of the CIA and an expert in terrorism and aviation security.

As you read, consider the following questions:

1. In Johnson's view, how does the bombing of Pan Am 103 demonstrate the limits of law enforcement?
2. According to statistics cited by the author, what percentage of international terrorist attacks in 1995 was directed against the United States?
3. How many terrorist hijackings have occurred since 1985, according to Johnson?

If the purpose of terrorism is to reach beyond its immediate victims and engender fear in the collective psyche, then an important part of any government's countermeasure strategy should be to keep the reality of terrorist activity in perspective. Unfortunately, that battle is not being fought, much less won.

Instead, the constant drumbeat from many government officials and private sector experts is that terrorism is on the rise. This view goes unchallenged because it parallels public perception. Everyone has a ready list of examples: the June 1996 attack on a U.S. military apartment complex in Saudi Arabia, the July 1996 pipe bomb incident at the Atlanta Olympics, and the December 1996 takeover of the Japanese ambassador's residence in Peru—to name a few.

But a careful analysis of data gathered by the CIA and the FBI paints a dramatically different picture. Public fears and government comments notwithstanding, terrorism is not on the rise.

TERRORIST INCIDENTS HAVE DECLINED

Terrorist incidents, both domestic and international, have fallen to levels not seen since the 1970s. Whether measured by the number of incidents, the number of fatalities, or the number of groups, raw statistics demonstrate that the level of terrorist violence has declined since the mid-1980s. In fact, the evidence suggests that terrorism was more widespread and more deadly during the 1980s.

International and domestic terrorist incidents have declined since 1987 and are approaching historic lows. Since reaching a peak of 665 international terrorist attacks in 1987, incidents fell to 440 in 1995. Even this number overstates the true level of activity because almost forty percent of the attacks were carried out by one group—the Kurdish Workers Party (PKK) inflicting terror on Turkey and Turkish interests (although the figures, as with all incidents classified as international terrorism, exclude purely internal activity such as terrorism in Turkey against Turkish targets).

Exclude the PKK and international terrorism in 1995 was at its lowest level in twenty-five years. What is more, preliminary statistics indicate that 1996 incidents plummeted to about 270, the lowest number since 1971.

TERRORISM IN THE 1980S WAS DEADLIER

Compare the number of current terrorist events with the fifteen-month period from June 1985 through September 1986—a typical period for terrorism in the eighties. On June 13, 1985, Hezbollah terrorists hijacked TWA flight 847 from Athens with

153 passengers on board. During the thirteen day standoff, Navy diver Robert Stethem was murdered.

On June 23, an on-board bomb blew up Air India flight 182 over the Atlantic. The plane crashed into the sea southwest of Ireland, and all 329 passengers, including nineteen Americans, died. In September, members of Abu Nidal tossed Soviet-made hand grenades into a café adjacent to the U.S. Embassy in Rome, injuring forty people.

A few weeks later (October 7), Palestinian terrorists hijacked the Italian cruise ship *Achille Lauro* and brutally murdered an elderly American passenger. Abu Nidal grabbed headlines again in December 1985 with a daring attack on passengers waiting to check-in for El Al flights at the international airports in Rome and Vienna.

The terrorist assaults continued unabated in 1986. On April 2 a bomb exploded on TWA flight 840 during its approach to Athens Airport. The blast tore through the fuselage, and four Americans—including a baby—were sucked from the plane. A radical Islamic group linked to Libya claimed credit. Three days later a device planted by Libyan agents ripped apart La Belle disco in West Germany; among the fatalities were two Americans; sixty-four other Americans were injured.

On September 5, four Palestinian terrorists seized Pan Am 73 with 389 passengers and crew on board. During a stopover in Pakistan, the plane's power supply failed and the terrorists started firing in panic. Twenty-two passengers died and more than 100 were wounded.

TERRORISM HAS BECOME LESS PREVALENT

The period from June 1995 to September 1996, by contrast, has seen fewer incidents, fewer casualties, fewer groups involved, and fewer countries sponsoring terrorism. Terrorists twice bombed U.S. military targets in Saudi Arabia, killing five U.S. personnel in November 1995 and nineteen soldiers in June 1996. Suicide bus bombings shook Israel and threatened the peace process during March, April, and May. But the level of activity is undeniably reduced.

In the United States, the contrast is even more pronounced. According to the FBI, fifty-one domestic attacks occurred in 1982, but 1995 saw only two acts of terrorism—the Oklahoma City bombing and a train derailment in Arizona—and, according to preliminary figures, only one (depending on how the black church fires in the south are classified) in 1996 (the Centennial Park blast).

Granted, the bombing of the federal building in Oklahoma represented the largest loss of life ever from a domestic terrorism incident, but no evidence supports the contention that it was part of a developing or emerging threat. The alleged culprits apparently worked in isolation, reportedly seeking to avenge the U.S. government raid at the Branch Davidian compound in Waco, Texas.

REASONS FOR THE DECLINE

Terrorism is down for several reasons: sound government policy, aggressive law enforcement, and the breakup of the Soviet Union.

Policy. The United States and its European allies in 1986 put aside differences and focused on toughening policies against terrorism. Subsequent actions included sanctions against Libya and Syria. Armed with new legal authority that allowed it to operate overseas, the FBI, with the help of the CIA, tracked down and arrested terrorists such as airplane hijacker Fawaz Younis. In addition, the U.S. government posted substantial rewards for information about terrorists and their plans.

Law enforcement. Governments around the world have also put more resources into fighting terrorists. Official facilities were hardened against attacks. Special operations military units were recruited and deployed. In 1972, for example, the German government lacked a special counterterrorism unit for handling hostage situations, a failing tragically evident during the fatal hostage drama at the Munich Olympics. By 1990, Germany and most other nations had created such forces.

As a case in point, Singapore's police strike force stormed a hijacked Malaysian passenger jet in March 1991, killed the four hijackers, and freed the 129 passengers on board without help from any other country. Like Singapore, many countries have been devoting more resources to intelligence and training. These efforts mean that terrorists are facing tougher opponents.

There are limits to what law enforcement and technology can accomplish. The case of Pan Am 103 is illustrative. Despite an impressive collaborative effort by U.S. and U.K. law enforcement and intelligence officials in documenting Libya's role in planning and attacking Pan Am 103, the culprits still have not been brought to trial. Unless Libya and other rogue states are held accountable for their heinous deeds, terrorists may be encouraged to believe they can murder at will and not be punished.

Domestically, the capabilities and effectiveness of U.S. law enforcement have improved as well. . . . All major cities now have units trained to handle explosive devices and hostage barricade situations. The United States, even as an open, free society, has not been an easy target for terrorists. Those that have attempted terrorist attacks in the United States generally have been captured, arrested, and jailed.

Fall of communism. The collapse of the Soviet Union eliminated a major source of training and support for international terrorism. Without the backing of Moscow, most nations sponsoring terrorism had to cut back on the financial support they provided. Cuba, for instance, no longer has the surplus funds to channel to Marxist groups in Latin America. Many such groups, therefore, subsequently put away their guns, went out of business, or dramatically curtailed their activities. Similarly, Iraq, Syria, and Libya can no longer count on Soviet patrons to protect them.

FATALITIES HAVE DECLINED

According to figures collected by the CIA, international terrorist attacks are not only less frequent, they are less lethal since the 1980s. The number of people wounded by terrorists around the world follows a similar pattern, with one important exception—April 1995, when the Tokyo subway system was attacked with poison gas.

Injuries and deaths from future incidents could increase in the future as weapons of mass destruction (that is, chemical, biological, or radiological) become easier for terrorists to make or obtain. That danger was highlighted in Tokyo, where Aum Shinrikyo, a cult devoted to an apocalyptic religious vision, sprayed a lethal nerve agent—sarin—into the Tokyo subway system. Had Aum Shinrikyo been more skilled, it could have murdered thousands of people and created a terrorist attack of truly cataclysmic proportions.

The Tokyo attack raises troubling issues. It demonstrated the vulnerability of public transportation systems to chemical and biological agents. It raised questions about the capabilities of nations to detect, deter, and manage the consequences of weapons of mass destruction used by terrorists. And it exposed the gaps in a government's ability to track and monitor terrorist groups.

These problems must be confronted, but they do not change the current reality of declining terrorist activity and should not be used to justify unfounded conclusions about the terrorist threat.

Despite the popular belief that U.S. citizens are often in danger from international terrorists, annual U.S. casualties from international terrorist attacks have been low. The data reveal only three exceptions: 1983, 1988, and 1993. The bombing of the Marine barracks in 1983 marked the deadliest terrorist attack ever directed against the United States. In 1988, most of the fatalities occurred when Pan Am 103 exploded over Lockerbie. The World Trade Center bomb in 1993 killed only a handful but hurt more than 1,000 people.

MASS CASUALTY ATTACKS ARE NOT A TREND

Is the world entering an era of fewer incidents and more casualties? Many pundits point to the Oklahoma City bombing, the Tokyo subway attack, and the World Trade Center bombing as evidence of a new trend in terrorism—mass casualties.

Yet terrorism designed to inflict mass casualties is not a new phenomenon. The history of the last thirty years records many instances where hundreds died in a single terrorist incident. For example, the deadliest attack ever against the United States occurred thirteen years ago, and mass casualty terrorist hijackings have become far less common in recent years.

The reality is that modern society remains vulnerable to depraved acts by individuals and groups willing to use violence for their own private purposes. But no evidence supports the conclusion that this is more of a problem now than in the past. As already mentioned, the availability of weapons of mass destruction could increase this risk but as yet that danger remains more a fear than a fact.

A CHANGE IN MOTIVATIONS

One factor that may lead to an increase in terrorist fatalities in the future is the apparent shift of terrorism from political statement to nihilistic act—terrorist activity directed against the government with a less obvious political tie.

Terrorism by definition has always had a political component. In addition, the very nature of terrorist activity is that it is used by those who believe they lack access to more traditional or legitimate means of political power to accomplish a political objective, such as the formation of a state in the case of the Palestine Liberation Organization.

But that traditional type of terrorism is on the decline, which will likely bring to the fore groups or individuals who don't appear to have a political agenda other than being alienated from the government.

The World Trade Center and the Oklahoma City bombings, for example, appear to have less to do with politics and more to do with revenge. The Oklahoma City defendants allegedly bombed the Murrah building to avenge the federal government's assault on the Branch Davidian compound in Waco. The World Trade Center attack reportedly was intended to punish the United States in part for supporting the government of Israel. Similarly, Aum Shinrikyo made no demands and had no stated goals when it put poison in the Tokyo subway system.

Terrorism Is No Longer Effective

The early, easy successes of terror tactics in the anti-imperial context [terrorism aimed at achieving independence for a colony] left everybody with a greatly inflated notion of what the technique could achieve against an established national government with local roots. A few decades later, the answer is clear: virtually nothing. Governments and armies that cannot "go home"—because they are already at home—simply do not give in to terrorism. . . .

"International" terrorism, which is meant to make governments elsewhere do something the terrorists want, has had even fewer successes.

Gwynne Dyer, St. Louis Post Dispatch, August 18, 1998.

If the nihilistic trend in terrorist activities continues, especially if coupled with more accessible weapons of mass destruction, it could play a part in changing the face of terrorism. But again, as yet, it should be noted, that the numbers do not support this conclusion.

When asked which country is the most frequent target of international terrorists, many Americans put the United States at the top. Data from the CIA and State Department demonstrate that this assumption was true only in the late 1960s and the early 1990s. From 1972 until 1991, most international terrorist attacks were not directed against Americans. During the Gulf War, the U.S. once again found itself the most frequent target. But by 1995 only 23 percent of international terrorist attacks were anti-United States.

Fewer Terrorist Groups

The number of international terrorist groups has dropped by almost 30 percent since 1987, according to statistics extrapolated from CIA data. Sixty-four known groups carried out terrorist attacks in 1987. By 1995, the number was down to thirty-seven. Fewer groups willing or able to carry out terrorist attacks provides one explanation for the drop in incidents.

The data also challenge the stereotype that most terrorist

groups are Islamic—although they are among the most deadly. Extrapolating statistics collected by the CIA since 1987 shows that Marxist-Leninist groups are the most common terrorists, but their numbers have dwindled since the collapse of the Soviet Union (from about thirty-five to fifteen). By contrast, the number of radical Islamic groups involved with terrorism (about ten) has been fairly consistent since 1987.

Means of attack. Government data also demonstrate that the number of incidents recorded by method of attack has decreased substantially since 1987. (This category differs from the number of overall incidents because an incident can have multiple methods of attack.)

Bombs and armed assault are the techniques most commonly used by terrorists. Fortunately, the number of explosive devices used in international terrorism is declining. As of 1995, the number of bombs used in terrorist attacks had reached its lowest point since 1971.

Even more dramatic is the reduction in terrorist and criminal activities directed against civil aviation. (Hijackings by terrorists are designed to secure a political end, not just to serve the hijacker's personal goals.) Only two terrorist hijackings have occurred since 1985—the commandeering of Air France during a stop in Algeria in December 1994 and the takeover of an Air Malaysia flight in spring 1991. (As of April 1997, it was unclear whether the November 1996 hijacking of an Ethiopian jet, resulting in a crash off the coast of the Comoros Islands, would be classified as a terrorist act.) And explosions on board commercial aircraft have not been a major problem since 1989.

The introduction of tighter security measures at airports around the world and growing international intolerance of hijackers are key factors in the observed decline. Unfortunately, civil aviation remains a tempting target to international terrorists, and the absence of incidents should not be used to justify more lenient security measures. . . .

THE FUTURE OF TERRORISM

Previous success in fighting terrorism does not ensure future security. The threat in recent years may have diminished, but terrorism is a dynamic, multifaceted phenomenon. As a tool of politically weak nations and groups, it is a relatively cheap alternative to military force. Moreover, the motives for terrorism vary—from politics to religion, from opportunism to nihilism. Since there is no single stereotype, nations must be prepared to meet a variety of threats. . . .

Responding to the terrorist threat in the mid-eighties, the United States learned that strong policy, international cooperation, and tough countermeasures hurt terrorists. It was true then and remains true today. In charting a course to deal with the future of terrorism, U.S. officials should take a careful look at the real nature of the threat and assemble a mix of strategies and tactics that are proactive and effective. Vigilance and preparation are a sound prescription for crafting an appropriate counterterrorism policy.

| "There is perhaps no greater threat to
... national security than the illicit
spread of mass destruction weapons."

WEAPONS OF MASS DESTRUCTION POSE A TERRORIST THREAT

Sam Nunn

The greatest threat to American and international security is weapons of mass destruction, contends Sam Nunn in the following viewpoint. He asserts that the use of these weapons by terrorist groups, such as the Aum Shinrikyo cult in Japan, will increase in coming years. Nunn argues that domestic and global strategies must be developed in order to reduce the threat. Nunn, a former U.S. senator from Georgia, is a Distinguished Professor at the Sam Nunn School of International Affairs at the Georgia Institute of Technology in Atlanta, Georgia.

As you read, consider the following questions:

1. In Nunn's view, what risks were created by the collapse of the Soviet Union?
2. What steps had Aum Shinrikyo taken to acquire and use weapons of mass destruction, according to the author?
3. According to Nunn, which international treaties and conventions should be used to fight mass destruction terrorism?

Reprinted from Sam Nunn, "The New Terror: Nutcakes with Nukes," *New Perspectives Quarterly*, Winter 1996, by permission of Blackwell Publishers.

As we stand at the threshold of the 21st century, there is perhaps no greater threat to this nation's, and indeed the world's, national security than the illicit spread of mass destruction weapons.

GLOBAL STABILITY HAS DECREASED

The end of the Cold War and the collapse of Soviet communism eliminated what many considered to be the gravest threat to world security and stability. We have moved from an era of high risk but also high stability to a climate of much lower risk but also much less stability. In many ways, the world is a far more unstable place today than it was a decade ago. Ethnic, religious, racial and political conflicts have led to an increasing level of violence and terrorism around the globe. It seems no place is immune today—not the marketplaces of Sarajevo, not the buses of Tel Aviv, not the subways of Tokyo or Paris, not the office buildings of New York or Oklahoma City. Zealotry in the name of a cause has created individuals and groups who are increasingly willing to do the unthinkable. Unfortunately, the ability to obtain weapons of mass destruction and carry out the unthinkable is increasingly coming within their grasp.

While the fall of the Soviet Union has certainly diminished the risk of a major war between the United States and a would-be challenger, it has also created new risks which could have an impact on the US. Never before has an empire collapsed leaving some 30,000 nuclear weapons, hundreds of tons of fissile material, at least 40,000 tons of chemical weapons, advanced biological weapons, huge stores of sophisticated conventional weapons and thousands of scientists with the knowledge to make all of the above. As the remnants of that empire struggle to achieve democratic reforms and build a free market economy, the challenge facing the Russians, and the entire world, is to ensure that the former Soviet Union does not become a vast supermarket for the most deadly instruments known to man. Unfortunately, there already are many prospective customers.

At the same time, the inexorable advance of science and communications has made the technology of these instruments available to an ever-widening audience. The formula for sarin and other chemical weapons is easily accessible over the Internet, as is information about biological weapons and even instructions as to how to make a nuclear device. The scenario of a terrorist group either obtaining or manufacturing and using a weapon of mass destruction is no longer the stuff of science fiction or adventure movies. It is a reality which has already come to pass, and one which, if we do not take appropriate measures, will increasingly threaten us in the future.

DEADLY ATTACKS IN JAPAN

In an event that was little noticed at the time outside of Japan, seven people died and over 500 were treated at hospitals when a mysterious vapor seeped into the open windows of an apartment complex in the city of Matsumoto on June 27, 1994. While some experts ultimately concluded that the vapor was the deadly nerve gas sarin, no group ever claimed credit for the incident and no arrests were made. As a result, the world paid little attention to the Matsumoto City incident.

The world was forced to pay attention, however, on the morning of March 20, 1995. On that day, at the height of the morning rush hour, several members of a religious cult which preached Armageddon between the US and Japan unleashed a sarin gas attack on the innocent civilian riders of the Tokyo subway system. The attack specifically targeted a central station in the heart of the city which served the major government agencies of the Japanese government.

Twelve persons were killed and over 5,000 injured. If the cult had crafted a more efficient delivery system prior to the attack, the death toll could easily have soared into the tens of thousands. Nevertheless, the relatively low death toll from this attack is a credit to the excellent work of the Japanese emergency response and health authorities. As a result of the investigation which followed the Tokyo attack, Japanese authorities were able to develop evidence that this cult had also carried out the earlier attack in Matsumoto City.

This cult, known as the Aum Shinrikyo, thus gained the distinction of becoming the first persons, other than a nation during wartime, to use chemical weapons on a major scale. The results of my Senate subcommittee investigation into the Japanese cult are deeply disturbing.

A DANGEROUS CULT

This was a group which, in furtherance of its religious and political goals, sought to acquire, and planned to use, some of the deadliest weapons known to man.

The Aum had built its own chemical manufacturing plant in which it produced such chemical agents as sarin and VX gas. They had also built a plant to develop biological weapons and may have developed such agents as botulina toxin and anthrax.

With over $1 billion in assets, money was no object for this group. They were willing to spend hundreds of thousands of dollars at a time on pieces of equipment to aid in their weaponization program. They were even willing to consider the cost of buying a nuclear weapon.

A CHRONOLOGY OF BIOLOGICAL TERRORISM		
Date and Site	Group	Incident
April 1997 Washington, D.C.	Counter Holocaust Lobbyists of Zion	Anthrax hoax
May 1992 Minnesota	Minnesota Patriot's Council	Planned to assassinate local law enforcement personnel with ricin
April 1990– March 1995 Japan	Aum Shinrikyo ("Supreme Truth")	Attempted various attacks with botulinum and anthrax
Mid-1980s Sri Lanka	Tamil secessionist group	Threatened to infect humans and crops with pathogens
August 1984 Oregon	Rajneeshee religious cult	Infected 751 people with salmonella in Wasco County
October 1984 Paris, France	Red Army Faction	French authorities find flasks of clostridium botulinum in terrorist safehouse
November 1970 Maryland	Weatherman organization	Sought to steal biological agents from Ft. Detrick to poison a city's water supply
1950s Kenya	Mau Mau	Used plant toxins to kill livestock

Sources: W. Seth Carus, "The Threat of Bioterrorism," *Strategic Forum* No. 127, September 1997; Joseph Douglass Jr. and Neil Livingstone, *America the Vulnerable*, 1987: "Army Tells of Plot to Steal Bacteria From Ft. Detrick," *The New York Times*, November 21, 1970.

The Aum's reach stretched literally around the world as they sought to fulfill the prophecies of their leader. The Aum had made extensive contacts in Russia in an effort to obtain military training, equipment and weapons, including laser weapons and nuclear weapons. They had traveled to Australia to mine uranium and to carry out tests with chemical agents. They even had members working here in the US attempting to obtain advanced technology and equipment to help them carry out their weapons production.

The Aum's office in the US was accessing and attempting to purchase sophisticated computer programs and equipment with potential military applications.

PREVENTING FUTURE ATTACKS

Despite all this activity, and despite the fact that the group's doomsday philosophy was primarily anti-US, the Aum was virtually unknown to US intelligence or law enforcement prior to the March 20 subway attack. In an age when we have witnessed two major terrorist attacks on targets in the US, anything other than constant vigilance in this area could have catastrophic consequences. Yet preventing groups such as the Aum from arising in the future and obtaining similar destructive capabilities is an extremely complex problem. It is not one that will be solved in one or two years. And it is not one that will yield to simple solutions.

It is a problem which will have to be fought on many fronts:

• We must develop a real awareness of the proliferation threat among the public, and, in particular, among the business and scientific communities which are the source of much of the precursor technology and materials which are vital to these groups.

• We must also beef up our human intelligence—and that means we must develop better coordination between intelligence and law enforcement, not only in this country but around the world.

• We must develop a global strategy, one which includes the countries of the former Soviet Union, and in particular Russia, to improve our capabilities worldwide to track and trace nuclear, chemical and biological material.

• We must concentrate on research and development efforts to greatly improve our capabilities to detail, trace and track weapons of mass destruction.

• We must enhance export control regimes worldwide and develop better technologies for border control.

• We must also make maximum use of arms control agreements such as START II and of international treaties and conventions such as the Non-Proliferation Treaty, the Biological Weapons Convention and the Chemical Weapons Convention.

• We must have a global coordinated effort against international organized crime and terrorism.

• We must intensify our cooperative efforts with the countries of the former Soviet Union to help them destroy their excess weapons and materials, improve their accounting and storage for those they do maintain, and help them find constructive employment alternatives for their scientists who would otherwise be tempted to sell their knowledge to Libya, North Korea or groups such as the Aum.

The spread of these awesome and awful devices of mass destruction has already reshaped the way we think about security. The challenge for the future will be how to shape a response as effective as our deterrent strategy during the Cold War.

| "The expectation of a massive chemical or biological attack is not based on actual terrorist incidents."

WEAPONS OF MASS DESTRUCTION DO NOT POSE A TERRORIST THREAT

Ehud Sprinzak

In the following viewpoint, Ehud Sprinzak contends that the threat of terrorist attacks using weapons of mass destruction has been overstated. He argues that, despite incidents such as the 1995 attack in a Tokyo subway station and the claims of government officials and politicians, conventional weapons such as car bombs continue to pose a greater danger than biological or chemical weapons. Sprinzak asserts that counterterrorism efforts need to focus on the real, not imagined, dangers. Sprinzak is a professor of political science at Hebrew University in Jerusalem.

As you read, consider the following questions:
1. According to Sprinzak, what three events convinced the top officials in the Defense Department that mass destruction terrorism was inevitable?
2. What book influenced President Clinton's views on terrorism, as stated by the author?
3. In the author's view, why is terrorism not about killing?

Reprinted from Ehud Sprinzak, "Terrorism: Real and Imagined," *The Washington Post*, August 19, 1998, by permission of the author.

Will we learn the right lessons from our failure to protect the U.S. embassies in Nairobi and Dar es-Salaam? [On August 7, 1998, simultaneous bombings at the U.S. embassies in Kenya and Tanzania killed a combined 224 people, including twelve Americans.] It's worth asking, because there is good reason to assume that the most relevant questions about this painful matter involve the Clinton administration's habit of worrying so much about terrorism conducted with weapons of mass destruction that it may be neglecting the ever-present risks of conventional terrorism.

No security service in the world can provide its clientele with impenetrable anti-terrorist protection. Security services are reasonably expected, however, to learn from experience, to identify dominant terrorism trends and to prepare for these contingencies.

CAR BOMBS ARE A DANGEROUS TREND

In both domestic and international terrorism there has been, since 1983, no more visible trend than car bombs—the kind used at the Marine barracks and American Embassy in Beirut, the World Trade Center, the federal building in Oklahoma City, the Israeli Embassy and the Jewish Community Center in Buenos Aires, and the Khobar Towers in Saudi Arabia.

A terrorist pattern has been systematically established: unclaimed car bombs. To believe that anti-American terrorists would refrain from using this tactic against U.S. embassies just because these commonly targeted symbols are not located in Tel Aviv, Riyadh or Kuwait City was naive and unprofessional.

That the CIA and the State Department were aware of the problem is evident from the *Washington Post*'s reports on the success of the agency's operatives in foiling several attacks on American embassies, and from Ambassador Prudence Bushnell's warning letters to her superiors in Washington about the embassy's security problems.

A PREOCCUPATION WITH MASS DESTRUCTION

Yet any elementary examination of America's counterterrorist policy in recent years reveals a preoccupation with unconventional terrorism and a steadily growing conviction that the next blow to the United States will involve the successful use of chemical, biological or radiological weapons. Three key events seem to have convinced the secretary of defense [William Cohen] and his top officials that mass destruction terrorism is almost inevitable: the 1995 nerve gas attack on a crowded Tokyo subway station by the Japanese millenarian cult Aum Shinrikyo;

the 1997 disclosure of alarming information about the former Soviet Union's massive bio-warfare program; and the disturbing discoveries about the extent of Saddam Hussein's hidden chemical and biological arsenal.

A fourth element was the impact on President Clinton of a popular science fiction novel. "The Cobra Event" describes in chilling detail a terrorist attack on New York City with a genetically engineered mix of smallpox and cold viruses. According to a report by William J. Broad and Judith Miller in the *New York Times* Aug. 7, 1998, Clinton became so fixated on the threat that he urged Speaker Newt Gingrich to read the book and made urgent preparations against an unconventional terror attack on the United States his personal project.

CHEMICAL AND BIOLOGICAL MATERIALS HAVE DRAWBACKS

It . . . needs to be recognized that there are major disadvantages to a terrorist in attempting to use chemical and biological (C/B) materials. First, if the material is to be effective, it must be disseminated in sufficient quantity to the target population—and it will be readily appreciated that because the target population is relatively widely dispersed, most of the C/B material will be lost by dilution into the atmosphere and very little will reach and affect the target population. Consequently, C/B terrorism represents a very inefficient and ineffective use of material—in sharp contrast to the use of explosives, where all the explosive is effective in the detonation.

Second, the local micro-meteorology will determine precisely how the C/B material spreads and the extent to which it is dispersed and diluted by atmospheric turbulence—a far cry from the military use of chemical warfare agents involving simultaneous release of large quantities of agent following a massive artillery or rocket attack. Consequently, a terrorist group will have far less certainty concerning whether a harmful concentration will indeed be achieved.

Graham S. Pearson, *Politics and the Life Sciences*, September 1996.

Billions of dollars have been sought by the administration since 1995 to prepare America for the shock of mass destruction terrorism, and Congress has been quick to provide the money. More important, the new emphasis has resulted in the replacement of traditional terrorism specialists by biologists and chemists. People who are respected scientists but who have never talked to or studied actual terrorists have become the president's top advisers on counterterrorism. Thus, while the agencies responsible for protecting U.S. citizens and installations abroad were sinking into monotonous routine work, America's most creative counterterrorism thinkers were devoting themselves exclusively to answering challenges posed by weapons of mass destruction.

THE THREAT IS OVERSTATED

The dual fallacy upon which the current frenzy is based was clear even before the explosions in East Africa. The expectation of a massive chemical or biological attack is not based on actual terrorist incidents, and it ignores preparations for a potential new wave of conventional terrorism. So far (and this includes the famed 1995 Japanese subway attack) the world has not witnessed any mass-casualty event resulting from unconventional terrorism. Most of the funds allocated to countering this threat have been committed on the basis of dubious conjecture and unsubstantiated worst-case scenarios.

In all this time, no serious thinking was devoted to what might happen when ordinary terrorists decided to resume their attacks and do what they know best: identify soft American targets, assemble conventional explosives and kill a large number of unprotected civilians.

There is, in fact, neither empirical evidence nor logical support for the growing conviction that a "post-modern" age of terrorism is about to dawn, an era afflicted by a large number of chemical and biological mass murderers.

FOCUS ON CONVENTIONAL TERRORISM

Terrorism, we must remember, is not about killing. Terrorism is a form of psychological warfare in which the killing of a relatively small number of innocent civilians is used to send a brutal message of hate and fear to hundreds of millions of people. Most known terrorists are unlikely to resort to weapons of mass destruction for the simple reason that they do not need them to accomplish their goals.

There are steps that can be taken now to ensure that there are no more Nairobis and Dar es-Salaams. The most important would be to rediscover conventional terrorism and reallocate the nation's counterterrorist resources accordingly.

"Information technology offers new
opportunities to terrorists."

TERRORISM AGAINST INFORMATION SYSTEMS IS A THREAT

Matthew G. Devost, Brian K. Houghton, and Neil Allen Pollard

In the following viewpoint, Matthew G. Devost, Brian K. Houghton, and Neil Allen Pollard assert that information terrorism—
acts of terrorism that target civilian and military society—is a
growing threat. The authors maintain that an increased reliance
on technology has made societies more vulnerable to information terrorism. They also contend that technological methods
have become more cost-effective to terrorists and hence more
appealing. Devost, Houghton, and Pollard are employees of Science Applications International Corporation, a high-technology
research and engineering company.

As you read, consider the following questions:

1. How do Devost, Houghton, and Pollard define political
   terrorism?
2. According to the authors, what are the dangers of labeling all
   malicious uses of computer systems terrorism?
3. What dilemmas are unique to combating information
   terrorism, in the view of the authors?

Excerpted from Matthew G. Devost, Brian K. Houghton, and Neil Allen Pollard,
"Information Terrorism: Political Violence in the Information Age," *Terrorism and Political
Violence*, Spring 1997. Reprinted by permission of Frank Cass, publishers.

The national security establishment is concerned with a new form of conflict: information warfare. Information warfare, loosely defined, is targeting the information and information systems that comprise and support civilian and military infrastructures of an adversary. Information warfare runs deeper than attacks on tanks and troops: an information warfare campaign can target and disrupt the information and networks that support crucial day-to-day workings of civilian, commercial and military systems (e.g., air traffic control, power grids, stock markets, international financial transactions, logistics controls, etc.) As US Director of Central Intelligence John Deutch stated, 'the electron is the ultimate precision-guided weapon'.

DEFINING INFORMATION TERRORISM

Information terrorism is an important subset of information warfare—perhaps more challenging to confront and respond to, because of the difficulty of determining the political agenda or sponsors of the perpetrators. Political terrorism is the systematic use of actual or threatened physical violence in the pursuit of a political objective, to create a general climate of public fear and destabilize a society, and thus influence the population or government policy. In a legal sense, information terrorism can be the intentional abuse of a digital information system, network or component toward an end that supports or facilitates a terrorist campaign or action. In this case, the system abuse would not necessarily result in direct violence against humans, although it may still incite fear. Information terrorism is the nexus between criminal information system fraud or abuse, and the physical violence of terrorism.

Information technology offers new opportunities to terrorists. A terrorist organization can reap low-risk, highly visible payoffs by attacking information systems. In an effort to attract the attention of the public, political terrorists perpetrate their acts with the media at the forefront of their strategy: this strategy calculus is based on the assumption that access to the communication structure is directly related to power. Believers in this assumption might target digital information systems in pursuit of political goals.

As technology becomes more cost-effective to terrorists—that is, its availability and potential for disruptive effects rise while its financial and other costs go down—terrorists will become more technologically oriented in tactics and strategies. In 1977, terrorist expert Robert Kupperman, then Chief Scientist of the US Arms Control and Disarmament Agency, recognized that increasing societal reliance upon technology changes the nature of the threat posed by terrorists:

> Commercial aircraft, natural gas pipelines, the electric power grid, offshore oil rigs, and computers storing government and corporate records are examples of sabotage-prone targets whose destruction would have derivative effects of far higher intensity than their primary losses would suggest. . . . Thirty years ago terrorists could not have obtained extraordinary leverage. Today, however, the foci of communications, production, and distribution are relatively small in number and highly vulnerable.

The criminal and subversive connotations of the term 'terrorist' have resulted in many acts of computer abuse being labeled 'information terrorism'. These acts have ranged from using personal information for extortion, to hacking into a network, to physical and/or electronic destruction of a digital information system. This is too simplistic a taxonomy for such a complex phenomenon.

TERRORISM IS POLITICAL

Labeling every malicious use of a computer system as 'terrorism' serves only to exacerbate confusion and even panic among users and the general public, and frequently hinders prosecution and prevention by blurring the motivations behind the crime. Furthermore, political crimes have vastly different implications for national security and defense policy than do other 'common' crimes. Terrorism is a *political* crime: an attack on the legitimacy of a specific government, ideology or policy. Hacking into a system to erase files out of sheer ego, or stealing information with the sole intent to blackmail, is nothing more than simple theft, fraud or extortion, and certainly is not an attack upon the general legitimacy of the government. Policy and methodology to counter crime depends a great deal upon criminal motivations; thus, clearer and more concise definitions of 'information terrorism' are needed if it is to be addressed by national security policy. Attacks on the legitimacy of a government or its policies are not 'common' criminal acts. The quasi-criminal, quasi-military nature of terrorism blurs the distinction between crime and warfare. Distinctions between law enforcement and military duties become equally blurred, and can be clarified only through coherent policy dictating those duties, based upon a clear view of the nature of the enemy.

The National Information Infrastructure (NII) and Global Information Infrastructure (GII) support financial, commercial and military information transfers for consumers, businesses and countries. Considering the presence of computers in modern society, it is not surprising that terrorists have occasionally targeted computer systems in the past. A 'PLO' virus was developed at the Hebrew University of Jerusalem in Israel; in Japan, groups have attacked the computerized control systems for commuter trains, paralyzing major cities for hours; the Italian Red Brigade's manifesto specified the destruction of computer systems and installations as an objective for 'striking at the heart of the state'. Sinn Fein supporters working out of the University of Texas, Austin, have posted sensitive details about British army intelligence installations, military bases and police stations in Northern Ireland on the Internet. Terrorism is a rapidly evolving and responsive phenomenon. Terrorist technology and tactics are sensitive to their target political cultures and have progressed at a rate commensurate with dominant military, commercial and social technologies.

THE METHODS OF INFORMATION TERRORISM

In the Information Age, there are two general methods by which a terrorist might employ an information terrorist attack: (1) when information technology (IT) is a target, and/or (2) when IT is the tool of a larger operation. The first method would target an information system for sabotage, either electronic or physical, thus destroying or disrupting the information system itself and any information infrastructure (e.g., power, communications, etc.) dependent upon the targeted technology. The second would manipulate and exploit an information system, altering or stealing data, or forcing the system to perform a function for which it was not meant (such as spoofing air traffic control).

TABLE 1. GENERAL METHODS FOR TERRORIST ATTACK IN INFORMATION AGE

		Target	
		Physical	Digital
Tool	Physical	(a) Conventional Terrorism (Oklahoma City Bombing)	(b) IRA attack on London Square Mile, 4 October 1992
	Digital	(c) Hacker spoofing an air traffice control system to bring down a plane	(d) Trojan horse in public switched network

In Table 1, cell (a) addresses 'traditional' terrorism (e.g., hijacking, bombings, assassinations, hostage taking, etc.). The authors consider cells (b), (c) and (d) to be information terrorism. Cell (b) represents a low-tech solution for a high-tech target (e.g., the IRA attack on Square Mile financial district of London). Cell (c) exploits information systems to wreak physical damage. Cell (d), digital tools against digital targets, exploits vulnerabilities in military, commercial and civilian/utility systems that rely on information technology. The authors believe cell (d) to be 'pure' information terrorism and likely the most difficult to detect and counter. The authors also believe that the equivalent of an 'electronic Pearl Harbor' certainly is possible and would have devastating results. In testimony to the Senate Permanent Subcommittee on Investigations, Director of Central Intelligence Deutch was prepared to prioritize information attacks as the second most worrisome threat to US national security, behind the threat posed by foreign nuclear, chemical and biological arms. However, there are more subtle forms of information terrorism (e.g., electronic fund theft to support terrorist operations, rerouting of arms shipments, etc.) which would still be political crimes, but perhaps more dangerous because they are less dramatic than a 'cyber-Chernobyl', and thus more difficult to detect, and can even appear as 'common' crimes.

Western democracies have always faced a dilemma in combating terrorism, of balancing civil liberty with civil security. Combating information terrorism encounters these common dilemmas as well as problems specific to the global character of information technology:

• How can the US national security establishment respond to the informational attacks of terrorists, when the terrorists hide behind a veil of digital anonymity?

• How much of information terrorism is a military concern and how much is within the jurisdiction of federal law enforcement?

• How can we better discern what is a political crime, and what is a 'common' crime (e.g., motivated by greed) in the infosphere?

• How can the national security establishment balance defending the National Information Infrastructure while being sensitive to civil 'cyber-liberties' and rights to privacy?

• How can a centralized, geographically focused national security establishment respond effectively to a digitally networked international enemy?

If for no other reason than to prevent an overreaction by the government, these concerns need to be addressed before we are confronted by an incident which scars America as deeply as the Oklahoma City bombing.

THE BENEFITS AND DRAWBACKS OF A MILITARY RESPONSE

These considerations certainly pose dilemmas, but they need not necessarily be intractable. The US national security establishment must be equipped to respond militarily to information terrorism. First, the military will always be a target of terrorism. Furthermore, the information terrorism attack may be state-sponsored and the first wave of a 'digital Pearl Harbor'. Origins of digital attacks are usually difficult to discover at first, and if the attack is indeed a precursor of peer or near-peer information warfare, a military response will be required.

However, democratic societies must carefully weigh the use of military forces in the prevention and countering of terrorism, even though their militaries may be targets of the attacks. By calling in the military to respond to conventional terrorist actions, the terrorists and their cause may achieve a degree of legitimacy. The terrorists' actions then have escalated from a criminal level to that of an 'enemy of the state'. This quandary can be avoided when countering information terrorists. There are no visible soldiers on the streets to heighten civilian anxieties when using digital attacks to counter the terrorists. The government's response, like that of the information terrorists, can be symmetrical: anonymous, fully networked and swift.

"There have been no organized attempts with a terrorist intent to disrupt [military and civilian] infrastructure."

THE THREAT OF INFORMATION TERRORISM HAS BEEN OVERSTATED

William Church, interviewed by John Borland

In the following viewpoint, William Church contends that information terrorism—attacks that target and exploit computer infrastructures—has not become a threat to modern society. He asserts that terrorists have not made the transition to cyber-weapons because they are more comfortable with physical weapons. He maintains that while there are hackers who infiltrate computer systems, they are more likely to be motivated by money rather than by a desire to undermine a government. Church is the founder of the Centre for Infrastructural Warfare Studies, an organization that is dedicated to discussing and analyzing threats to the information infrastructure.

As you read, consider the following questions:

1. According to Church, who is the leader in information weaponry?
2. In Church's view, what is one possible scenario for information terrorism?
3. How many professional computer hackers/crackers exist, as cited by Church?

Abridged from John Borland, "Analyzing the Threat of Cyberterrorism," *Techweb*, September 23, 1998, www.techweb.com. Reprinted by permission of CMP Media Inc.'s *Techweb*.

William Church is managing director of a San Francisco company that tracks computer break-ins, power failures, and telephone outages around the world, then turns these data points into analyses of weaknesses in national infrastructures.

THREATS TO INFRASTRUCTURES

Church, a former U.S. Army Intelligence officer, founded the Centre for Infrastructural Warfare Studies (CIWARS) two years ago to write a report on U.S. infrastructure vulnerabilities. The report was funded by a private group called the Internet Science Education Project and used as a reference by the presidential Commission on Critical Infrastructure Protection. . . .

Church's research focuses on attacks against infrastructure facilities, ranging from e-mail bombs to cracking attacks meant to shut down vital infrastructure facilities such as power stations or telephone switches. He says these weapons have been used routinely by individual hackers, and to some extent by organized crime and national governments. But terrorists have yet to make the transition to cyberweapons, he says.

TechWeb Internet asked Church why terrorists have been so slow to move their operations online.

A SLOW TRANSITION

John Borland: William Church, you say terrorists haven't really made the transition to information weapons yet. Why not?

William Church: For terrorists to make this transition, there have to be a number of factors brewing or building. First, they must understand the use of the weapon, and they must trust the use of the weapon. Normally, terrorists only make that trust or that leap if they've built it themselves, they've experimented with it, and they know for a fact it will work. Then they're willing to try their one-time shot at using this type of weapon.

They normally don't like to experiment. That's why overall, weapons proliferate from states to terrorists. They get to see how it actually works.

At this point, states really haven't gotten into the use of this kind of weapon?

Only the United States. The United States is probably the leader of this market, and things are definitely not proliferating outside of the United States.

The other transition point is mentality, or mental mindset, you might say. They must know it, they must trust it, but more importantly it has to feel right to them.

If you look at the Irish Republican Army, which was probably the closest before they made peace, they were on the verge of it.

They had computer-oriented cells. They could have done it. They were already attacking the infrastructure by placing real or phony bombs in electric plants, to see if they could turn off the lights in London. But they were still liking the feel of physical weapons, and trusting them.

No Organized Attempts

But at this point none of the groups that are conventionally defined as terrorist groups have used information weapons against the infrastructure?

No.

And for me to answer that, we really need to qualify, we need to separate the hyperbole from the reality. Even though the U.S. government has cited the Sri Lankan freedom fighters liberation groups as using the first cyberterrorist weapons, that is nonsense. It was e-mail attacks. That is harassment, that is not terrorism.

So yes, there have been no organized attempts with a terrorist intent to disrupt the infrastructure. There have been disruptions of the infrastructure, for sure. But not a threat motivation organized around a group or even an individual with that exact intent.

There are a few qualifications. There have been individuals like the Swedish hacker that turned off the 911 system in Florida. But there's no proof that he had hostile intent.

Are these the sort of weapons that make sense, say, for a terrorist group like bin Ladin's to use? Or is the visual impact of a bomb, of a building being bombed, a more natural fit for groups like that?

Well, yes, you sort of hit the nail on the head. But we should never discount the fact there might be a terrorist group that would make this transition and not go for visuals, that is, wants to do a more subtle approach. But today, the terrorist groups we're dealing with, I think, are bound to visuals.

A possible scenario would be an internal terrorist group that didn't want to alienate the population by death, but still wanted to make a statement. Now, that's possible that would materialize.

Governments and Cyberweapons

Do you think it's more likely terrorist groups will go in this direction first, or actual governments will use these sort of weapons, or organized crime will? Who's most likely to make this kind of transition first?

As I've stressed, usually what happens is it starts with the state. So the United States has already used it, according to Congressional testimony by the CIA director, George Tenet. According to my reports, what I've read, he has testified the United States has used information operations—which is usually a military euphemism for these types of activities—to disrupt the bank account of an Arab businessperson. Who, at the time, I thought was bin Ladin. The purpose was to disrupt the organization, to disrupt the money-transfer process.

But yes, we're seeing governments use information operations, but especially in espionage. But only the United States that we know of today. So it's coming. It's slowly creeping up on us.

THE HUMAN ELEMENT HAS BEEN IGNORED

A commonly offered scenario [for cyberterrorism] involves the air traffic system. The world's air traffic control system is highly computerized. The "terrorist" either obtains control of the system or alters the system in such a fashion that airplanes are flown into each other, resulting in mass death.

This scenario requires that the entire human element and the structure of the rules involving the control of aircraft are ignored. The computers used in the air traffic control system do not control anything. They merely provide an aid to the human controller. Even if he/she were deceived by the computer, there are other human beings in the loop. A basic tenet in pilot training is "situational awareness". From the first day of training, pilots are taught to be aware of not only their location, direction and altitude, but those of all other aircraft. Pilots routinely catch errors committed by air traffic controllers. It is the spectacular human failures that result in aircraft collisions. Further, the "rules of the road" for aircraft operations anticipate the complete failure of the air traffic control system. In fact, the rules are designed to work where there is no air traffic control at all!

Mark M. Pollitt, "Cyberterrorism: Fact or Fancy?" Found at http://www.cs.georgetown.edu/~denning/infosec/pollitt.html.

You make a distinction between individual hackers and groups that are essentially defined as terrorist groups, right?

It's not that a terrorist group couldn't use an individual hacker. But we have no record today of a terrorist group doing this. When I say we, I'm talking about my organization. The government might, but in all of our interviews and all of our research, we haven't found this.

THE ROLE OF HACKERS

There is cracking talent out there on the market now?

According to our studies. And let me stress, these are purely our studies. We've done this by surveying each one of our offices and asking them based on their expertise and working with [Computer Emergency Response Teams] to look at different kinds of attacks and say how they think they are professional.

We think there are somewhere around a thousand professional hackers/crackers in the world. I need to draw a line here. These are people with hard-core skills. They know exactly what they're doing. They use a combination of social-engineering skills, they're not afraid to get up close and personal with the target and social engineer, and at the same time use their programming skills. These are highly trained professionals and are way out of the age bracket of the teenage hacker. These people are very difficult to stop. They'll come at you in ten different ways, not just trying to get through a firewall. They'll steal a password, they'll put honey pots out there to trap passwords, they'll do anything.

That's probably the biggest threat. The good news is they're purely financially motivated today. That means they're basically after stealing money, or doing some kind of corruption around money.

So these aren't people who would try to undermine the infrastructure for political or whatever reasons?

There's no evidence of that today. I'm sure if you paid them enough that they might do that.

PERIODICAL BIBLIOGRAPHY

The following articles have been selected to supplement the diverse views presented in this chapter. Addresses are provided for periodicals not indexed in the *Readers' Guide to Periodical Literature*, the *Alternative Press Index*, the *Social Sciences Index*, or the *Index to Legal Periodicals and Books*.

William Broad	"When a Cult Turns to Germ Warfare," *New York Times*, May 26, 1998.
John Deutch	"Think Again: Terrorism," *Foreign Policy*, Fall 1997.
Issues and Controversies On File	"International Terrorism," October 9, 1998. Available from Facts On File News Services, 11 Penn Plaza, New York, NY 10001-2006.
David Johnston and Philip Shenon	"A Scorecard on Terrorist Attacks," *New York Times*, August 9, 1998.
David E. Kaplan	"Terrorism's Next Wave," *U.S. News & World Report*, November 17, 1997.
David E. Kaplan	"Terrorism Threats at Home," *U.S. News & World Report*, December 29, 1997–January 5, 1998.
Walter Laquer	"Terror's New Face: The Radicalization and Escalation of Modern Terrorism," *Harvard International Review*, Fall 1998. Available from PO Box 380226, Cambridge, MA 02238-0226.
John Leifer	"Apocalypse Ahead," *Washington Monthly*, November 1997.
Wayman C. Mullins and Tomas C. Mijares	"The Restructuring of Europe: Projected Terrorist Trends in the Twenty-First Century," *Journal of Contemporary Criminal Justice*, February 1995. Available from Sage Publications, 2455 Teller Rd., Thousand Oaks, CA 91320.
Bruce W. Nelan	"The Price of Fanaticism," *Time*, April 3, 1995.
Douglas Pasternak and Bruce B. Auster	"Terrorism at the Touch of a Keyboard," *U.S. News & World Report*, July 13, 1998.
Joseph F. Pilat	"Chemical and Biological Terrorism After Tokyo: Reassessing Threats and Response," *Politics and the Life Sciences*, September 1996.
Ehud Sprinzak	"The Great Superterrorism Scare," *Foreign Policy*, Fall 1998.
Jose Vegar	"Terrorism's New Breed," *Bulletin of the Atomic Scientists*, March/April 1998.
Douglas Waller	"Onward Cyber Soldiers," *Time*, August 21, 1995.

WHAT MOTIVATES TERRORISTS?

CHAPTER PREFACE

With some acts of terrorism, the perpetrator is among the casualties. While in some cases the terrorist's death may have been an accident, in other situations he or she has deliberately set out to die amidst the intended victims—to be a "suicide bomber." This situation occurs most frequently among Islamic terrorists in Israel and the occupied territories, and it raises the question of what motivates terrorists to not just blow up a bus or a marketplace but to kill themselves in the process.

According to some observers, Palestinian suicide bombers are motivated by two thoughts: avenging the deaths of other Palestinians and achieving a martyr status which many Muslims believe will guarantee their entrance into Paradise. Beverly Milton-Edwards, a specialist in Palestinian politics, writes: "A religious conviction that the death of innocents should be avenged, . . . motivated [some terrorists] to adopt the tactic of suicide bombing." Martyrdom has its place of honor in Islam, but suicide is forbidden. Thus, some people argue that the bombers do not consider themselves to be suicidal but instead view their actions as examples of religious battle, justified by passages in the Koran. The *Free Arab Voice* asserts, "Whatever one may think of [a July 1997] bombing in Jerusalem, it wasn't suicide. . . . For better or for worse, the two martyrs were willing to die for their beliefs."

Understandably, this explanation for suicide bombings does not sit well with everyone. Some critics argue that the belief in martyrdom is dangerous and that Palestinian suicide bombings need to be seen as immoral acts of violence against Israel, rather than examples of deep religious fervor. Others disagree with the motivation but assert that understanding the thought processes of these terrorists may make it easier for Israel to fight terrorism. According to Louis Rene Beres, a professor at Purdue University, "Once Israel understands that terrorism is a kind of religious sacrifice, it will be on the way to effective counterterrorism."

While religious conviction is a motive for terrorism, it is not the only one. In the following chapter, the authors propose several factors that motivate terrorists to carry out deadly acts of protest.

"Religious terrorists embrace a total
ideological vision of an all-out
struggle to resist secularization."

RELIGIOUS FANATICISM MOTIVATES TERRORISTS

Magnus Ranstorp

In the following viewpoint, Magnus Ranstorp contends that religious fanaticism is a principal motivation for terrorism. He asserts that followers of various faiths, such as Islam, Judaism, and Japanese cults, are often led to perform terrorist acts. Ranstorp argues that religious terrorism is a type of political violence that is motivated by a sense of spiritual crisis and a reaction to social and political changes. According to Ranstorp, these terrorist groups are responding to threats of secularization inside and outside their countries. Ranstorp is a research associate at the Center for the Study of Terrorism and Political Violence at the University of St. Andrew's in Scotland and the author of *Hizb'allah in Lebanon: The Politics of the Western Hostage Crisis*.

As you read, consider the following questions:

1. According to Ranstorp, what proportion of recorded incidents of terrorism between 1970 and July 1995 were due to religious extremist movements?
2. Who is Islam's *jihad* fought against, as stated by the author?
3. According to the author, how are the Jewish Kach and Islamic Hamas organizations similar?

Excerpted from Magnus Ranstorp, "Terrorism in the Name of Religion," *Journal of International Affairs* and the Trustees of Columbia University in the City of New York. Footnotes in the original have been omitted in this reprint.

Far afield from the traditionally violent Middle East, where religion and terrorism share a long history, a surge of religious fanaticism has manifested itself in spectacular acts of terrorism across the globe. This wave of violence is unprecedented, not only in its scope and the selection of targets, but also in its lethality and indiscriminate character. Examples of these incidents abound: in an effort to hasten in the new millennium, the Japanese religious cult Aum Shinrikyo released sarin nerve gas on the Tokyo underground in June 1995; the followers of Sheikh 'Abd al-Rahman's al-Jama'a al-Islamiyya, caused mayhem and destruction with the bombing of Manhattan's World Trade Center and had further plans to blow up major landmarks in the New York City area; and two American white supremacists carried out the bombing of a U.S. Federal Building in Oklahoma City. All are united in the belief on the part of the perpetrators that their actions were divinely sanctioned, even mandated, by God. Despite having vastly different origins, doctrines, institutions and practices, these religious extremists are unified in their justification for employing sacred violence, whether in efforts to defend, extend or avenge their own communities, or for millenarian or messianic reasons. This viewpoint seeks to explore the reasons for the contemporary rise in terrorism for religious motives and to identify the triggering mechanisms that bring about violence out of religious belief in both established and newly formed terrorist groups.

THE ESCALATION OF RELIGIOUS TERRORISM

Between the mid-1960s and the mid-1990s, the number of fundamentalist movements of all religious affiliations tripled worldwide. Simultaneously, as observed by Bruce Hoffman, there has been a virtual explosion of identifiable religious terrorist groups from none in 1968 to today's level, where nearly a quarter of all terrorist groups active throughout the world are predominantly motivated by religious concerns. Unlike their secular counterparts, religious terrorists are, by their very nature, largely motivated by religion, but they are also driven by day-to-day practical political considerations within their context-specific environment. This makes it difficult for the general observer to separate and distinguish between the political and the religious sphere of these terrorist groups.

Nowhere is this more clear than in Muslim terrorist groups, as religion and politics cannot be separated in Islam. For example, Hizb'allah or Hamas operate within the framework of religious ideology, which they combine with practical and precise political action in Lebanon and Palestine. As such, these groups embrace simultaneously short-term objectives, such as the release of imprisoned members, and long-term objectives, such as continuing to resist Israeli occupation of their homelands and liberating all "believers." This is further complicated with the issue of state-sponsorship of terrorism: Religious terrorist groups often became cheap and effective tools for specific states in the advancement of their foreign policy political agendas. They may also contain a nationalist-separatist agenda, in which the religious component is often entangled with complex mixture of cultural, political and linguistic factors. The proliferation of religious extremist movements has also been accompanied by a sharp increase in the total number of acts of terrorism since 1988, accounting for over half of the 64,319 recorded incidents between 1970 and July 1995. This escalation by the religious terrorists is hardly surprising given the fact that most of today's active groups worldwide came into existence very recently. They appeared with a distinct and full-fledged organizational apparatus. They range from the Sikh Dal Khalsa and the Dashmesh organizations, formed in 1978 and 1982 respectively and the foundation of the Shi'ite Hizb'allah movement in Lebanon in 1982, to the initial emergence of the militant Sunni organizations, Hamas and Islamic Jihad, in conjunction with the 1987 outbreak of the Palestinian Intifada as well as the establishment of the Aum Shinrikyo in the same year.

CHANGES IN RELIGIOUS TERRORISM

The growth of religious terrorism is also indicative of the transformation of contemporary terrorism into a method of warfare and the evolution of the tactics and the techniques used by various groups, as a reaction to vast changes within the local, regional and global environment over the last three decades. These changes can be seen in numerous incidents, from the spate of hijackings by secular Palestinian terrorists and the mayhem of destruction caused by left- and right-wing domestic terrorists throughout Europe, to the current unprecedented global scope and level of religious extremism.

The evolution of today's religious terrorism neither has occurred in a vacuum nor represents a particularly new phenomenon. It has, however, been propelled to the forefront in the post-Cold War world, as it has been exacerbated by the explosion of ethnic-religious conflicts and the rapidly approaching new millennium. The accelerated dissolution of traditional links of social and cultural cohesion within and between societies with the current globalization process, combined with the historical legacy and current conditions of political repression, economic inequality and social upheaval common among disparate religious extremist movements, have all led to an increased sense of fragility, instability and unpredictability for the present and the future. The current scale of religious terrorism, unprecedented in militancy and activism, is indicative of this perception that their respective faiths and communities stand at a critical historical juncture: Not only do the terrorists feel the need to preserve their religious identity, they also see this time as an opportunity to fundamentally shape their future. There are a number of overlapping factors that have contributed to the revival of religious terrorism in its modern and lethal form at the end of the millennium. . . .

THE REASONS FOR RELIGIOUS TERRORISM

A survey of the major religious terrorist groups in the 1990s would reveal that almost all experience a serious sense of crisis in their environment, which has led to an increase in the number of groups recently formed and caused an escalation in their activities. This crisis mentality in the religious terrorist's milieu is multifaceted, at once in the social, political, economic, cultural, psychological and spiritual sphere. At the same time, it has been greatly exacerbated by the political, economic and social tumult, resulting in a sense of spiritual fragmentation and radicalization of society experienced worldwide in the wake of the end of the Cold War and the extremist's "fear of the forced march toward 'one worldism.'" Yet, this sense of crisis, as a perceived threat to their identity and survival, has been present to varying degrees throughout history. It has led to recurring phases of resurgence in most faiths. In these revivals, the believers use the religion in a variety of ways: they take refuge in the religion, which provides centuries-old ideals by which to determine goals; they find physical or psychological sanctuary against repression; or they may use it as a major instrument for activism or political action. Thus, religious terrorists perceive their actions as defensive and reactive in character and justify them in this way. Islam's jihad, for example, is essentially a defensive doctrine, religiously sanctioned by leading Muslim theologians, and fought against perceived aggressors, tyrants and "wayward Muslims." In its most violent form, it is justified as a means of last resort to prevent the extinction of the distinctive identity of the Islamic community against the forces of secularism and modernism. As outlined by Sheikh Fadlallah, the chief ideologue of

Hizb'allah: "When Islam fights a war, it fights like any other power in the world, defending itself in order to preserve its existence and its liberty, forced to undertake preventive operations when it is in danger." This is echoed by Sikh extremists, who advocate that, while violence is not condoned, when all peaceful means are exhausted, "you should put your hand on the sword." The defensive character of protecting one's faith through religious violence is also evident in the Sikhs' fear of losing their distinct identity in the sea of Hindus and Muslims. In the United States, the paranoid outlook of white supremacist movements is driven by a mixture of racism and anti-Semitism, as well as mistrust of government and all central authority. This sense of persecution is also visible among the Shi'ites as an historically dominant theme for 13 centuries, manifested in the annual Ashura processions by the Lebanese Hizb'allah, commemorating the martyrdom of Imam Husayn. This event and mourning period have been used as justification and as a driving force behind its own practice of martyrdom through suicide attacks.

Striking Blood

Lurie's World. Reprinted by permission of Cartoonews International Syndicate.

Other than a few strictly millenarian or messianic groups (such as Aum Shinrikyo or some Christian white supremacist movements), almost all the contemporary terrorist groups with a distinct religious imperative are either offshoots or on the fringe of broader movements. As such, the militant extremists' decisions to organize, break away or remain on the fringe are, to a large extent, conditioned by the political context within which they operate. Their decisions are shaped by doctrinal differences, tactical and local issues, and the degree of threat that they perceive secularization poses to their cause. This threat of secularization may come either from within the movements themselves and the environment with which they come into contact, or from outside influences. If the threat is external, it may amplify their sense of marginality within, and acute alienation from, society. It may also fuel the need to compensate for personal sufferings through the radical transformation of the ruling order. The internal threat of secularization is often manifest in a vociferous and virulent rejection of the corrupt political parties, the legitimacy of the regime, and also the lackluster and inhibited character of the existing religious establishment. Thus, religious terrorism serves as the only effective vehicle for political opposition. As explained by Kach's leader, Baruch Marzel, "[w]e feel God gave us in the six-day war, with a miracle, this country. We are taking this present from God and tossing it away. They are breaking every holy thing in this country, the Government, in a very brutal way." Similarly, as voiced by the late Palestinian Islamic Jihad leader, Fathi al-Shaqaqi, with reference to the Gaza-Jericho agreement between the Palestine Liberation Organization (PLO) and Israel: "Arafat has sold his soul for the sake of his body and is trying to sell the Palestinian people's soul in return for their remaining alive politically." The religious terrorist groups' perception of a threat of secularization from within the same society is also manifest in the symbolism used in the selection of their names, indicating that they have an absolute monopoly of the truth revealed by God. It is, therefore, not surprising that some of the most violent terrorist groups over the last decade have also adopted names accordingly: Hizb'allah (Party of God), Aum Shinrikyo (The Supreme Truth), and Jund al-Haqq (Soldiers of Truth). These names also endow them with religious legitimacy, historical authenticity and justification for their actions in the eyes of their followers and potential new recruits. They also provide valuable insight into their unity of purpose, direction and degree of militancy, with names like Jundallah (Soldiers of God), Hamas (Zeal), Eyal (Jewish Fighting Organization) and Le Groupe Islamique Armé (Armed Islamic Group, GIA), which promise unabated struggle and sacrifice.

SECULARIZATION IS CONSIDERED A THREAT

The threat of secularization from foreign sources is also the catalyst for springing religious terrorists into action. Intrusion of secular values into the extremists' own environment and the visible presence of secular foreign interference provoke self-defensive aggressiveness and hostility against the sources of these evils. This is especially true against perceived colonalism and neo-colonialism by western civilizations or against other militant religious faiths. These defensive sentiments are often combined with the visible emergence and presence of militant clerical leaders. Such leaders have more activist and militant ideologies than the mainstream movement from which they have emerged as either clandestine instruments or breakaway groups. It is often the case that these clerical ideologues and personalities act as a centrifugal force in attracting support, strengthening the organizational mechanisms and in redefining the methods and means through terrorism. At the same time, they provide theological justification, which enables their followers to pursue the sacred causes more effectively and rapidly. The so-called spiritual guides, who ultimately overlook most political and military activities while blessing acts of terrorism, can be found in almost all religious terrorist groups: Examples include Hizb'allah's Sheikh Fadlallah, Hamas' Sheikh Yassin, the militant Sikh leader Sant Bhindranwale and Aum Shinrikyo's leader, Shoko Asahara. . . .

BATTLING SECULARIZATION

In many ways, religious terrorists embrace a total ideological vision of an all-out struggle to resist secularization from within as well as from without. They pursue this vision in totally uncompromising holy terms in literal battles between good and evil. Ironically, there is a great degree of similarity between the stands of the Jewish Kach and Islamic Hamas organizations: Both share a vision of a religious state between the Jordan River and the Mediterranean Sea, a xenophobia against everything alien or secular which must be removed from the entire land, and a vehement rejection of western culture. The distinction between the faithful and those standing outside the group is reinforced in the daily discourse of the clerics of these terrorist groups. The clerics' language and phraseology shapes the followers' reality, reinforcing the loyalty and social obligation of the members to the group and reminding them of the sacrifices already made, as well as the direction of the struggle. In this task, many religious terrorist groups draw heavily upon religious symbolism and rituals to reinforce the sense of collectiveness. Examples of this emphasis on collectivity include the local reputation of the fighters of the underground military wing of Hamas, famous for never surrendering to arrest, the growth of

Hamas martyrology, which lionizes martyrs with songs, poems and shrines, and the frequent symbolic burning and desecration of Israeli and American flags by several Islamic groups across the Middle East. This collectiveness is also reinforced by the fact that any deviation or compromise amounts to treachery and a surrender of the principles of the religious faith is often punishable by death. . . .

This viewpoint has sought to demonstrate that, contrary to popular belief, the nature and scope of religious terrorism is anything but disorganized or random, but rather driven by an inner logic common among diverse groups and faiths who use political violence to further their sacred causes. The resort to terrorism by religious imperative is also not a new phenomenon, but rather deeply embedded in the history and evolution of the faiths. Religions have gradually served to define the causes and the enemies as well as the means, methods and timing of the violence itself.

"Twentieth-century developments
have created a climate favoring the
resort to violence by a variety of
politically alienated individuals and
groups."

POSTWAR DEVELOPMENTS MOTIVATE TERRORISTS

Joseba Zulaika and William A. Douglass

Political and social developments after World War II have contributed to the rise in terrorism, argue Joseba Zulaika and William A. Douglass in the following viewpoint. They maintain that factors such as decolonization, the Cold War, and the development of a postindustrial, urban society has exacerbated a sense of alienation among many groups of people. This feeling of loneliness and helplessness can manifest itself in terrorism, the authors assert. Zulaika and Douglass are the authors of *Terror and Taboo: The Follies, Fables, and Faces of Terrorism*, the book from which this viewpoint is taken.

As you read, consider the following questions:

1. According to the authors, what problems did new countries face following the end of colonization?
2. What led to the creation of the "global village," according to Zulaika and Douglass?
3. In the authors' views, what are three ways to cope with the problems of the late twentieth century?

In the mid-1970s, terrorism strikes everywhere and is mush-rooming at an alarming rate. On its own terms, terrorism has lit-erally been a smash hit. . . . The little guys and the little groups make the big difference.

—F.J. Hacker, *Crusaders, Criminals, Crazies*

In 1933, Jacob Hardman published an article on terrorism in *The Encyclopedia of the Social Sciences*. He argued that terrorism was for years an accepted tenet of anarchism, and its fullest expression was to be found in the Russian revolutionary movement of late last century. There was an attempt to revive terrorism at the beginning of the present one, but various factors "made terrorism appear outmoded as a revolutionary method.... The rising mass movement and the spread of nation-wide economic and political strikes made terror irrelevant and unnecessary." Apart from brief episodes, terrorism was simply an antiquated mode of struggle that had ceased to exist. But after World War II it again became fashionable (due to the political struggles of Israel, Kenya, Vietnam, Algeria, etc.). There is no small irony in this brief history of terrorism, in that those decades blessed with the interlude witnessed the emergence of Stalin and Hitler and experienced the two World Wars that resulted in some 70 million fatalities. Seemingly, when there is unbridled real combat, there is less need for a ritual surrogate.

THE REASONS FOR THE RISE OF TERRORISM

There are several interrelated factors that contributed to the emergence of terrorism in its modern guise. All were set in motion by certain events and developments of World War II and its immediate aftermath, but the mix of elements required about two decades of fermentation before attaining full strength as terrorist brew by the late 1960s and early 1970s.

First, there was the process of decolonization, which created a plethora of new states around the globe. The seemingly enlightened leadership of each promised to guide an independent "people" to either democratic paradise or socialist utopia. The initial euphoria of national liberation obfuscated or trivialized such fundamental problems as the dangers of internal ethnic and sectarian divisions, economic underdevelopment, and the authoritarian traditions characteristic of most of the new countries. Inevitably, over time euphoria gave way to cynicism as the failures became increasingly obvious and as self-serving ruling elites became ever more entrenched.

Second, in the postwar period the world became polarized

into two spheres of influence, each dominated by mutually antagonistic superpowers. The Cold War confrontation quickly lapsed into gridlock sustained by the balance of nuclear threat. The fear of escalation into nuclear annihilation all but ruled out conventional warfare, at least on a major scale. Consequently, the real struggle was fought over "the hearts and minds" of the uncommitted (the shrewdest of whom became adept at playing one side off against the other). Both superpowers encouraged foreign students by the tens of thousands to attend their universities in the hope of inculcating future generations of world leaders with their respective political philosophies. Both launched outreach programs designed to help underdeveloped countries to modernize, which thereby enmeshed them within the transnational economy dominated by the benefactor. On occasion each probed the limits of the other's power by sponsoring military insurrections, the dirty little wars of the guerrilla variety so characteristic of the last fifty years. In their relentless pursuit of client-states, both superpowers developed a clear double standard in which the gap between the propaganda and actions within their domestic versus their foreign policies became patently apparent.

Third, the postwar world experienced a variety of demographic and socioeconomic developments that exacerbated its difficulties. A population explosion negated many of the efforts to improve living standards. At the same time, the spread of the commitment to mass education and communication led to the creation of the "global village," in which everyone's frame of reference was expanded enormously. In the process most of the citizens of the planet bought into modern consumerism as the desired life style against which to measure one's personal success. Even the more developed societies, with their modest population growths, struggled to meet the rising expectations and absorb the capacities of an increasingly trained and educated work force. The enhanced efficiency of modernized agriculture displaced huge segments of the rural populace; developments in heavy industry likewise made redundant many of the heirs of the industrial revolution. The resulting postindustrial, urban society has become fraught with uncertainty regarding the capacity to meet human needs and aspirations without destroying the ecological balance of the planet in the process.

GROWING ALIENATION

With all of the foregoing factors put in motion, by the late 1960s and early 1970s there was ample reason for any citizen of Planet Earth to feel a degree of personal alienation. We all seemed to be caught up in a web of forces far beyond our control. The political leadership of every country appeared incapable of dealing with the plethora of social, economic, and ecological issues of an increasingly complicated world. Expansion of every individual's personal frame of reference seemed to shrivel and undermine the intimate web of traditional values as articulated through family and neighborhood, church and community. Interaction between human beings became increasingly electronical and technological rather than of the face-to-face variety. Works like Phillip Slater's *The Pursuit of Loneliness* captured the essence of the combination of alienation and anomie seemingly inherent in the modern condition.

TURNING POINTS IN WORLD WAR II

After World War II, terrorism swung back to a strategy of the "outs" versus the "ins." Two clusters of events from the war years were particularly significant for inspiring the ethno-nationalist aspirations that have been so important over the last half-century. First, when the British were defeated at Singapore in February 1942 and the Americans surrendered at Corregidor in May 1942, the myth of Western invincibility was shattered. Second, the Atlantic Charter, signed by Churchill and Roosevelt in August 1941, turned out to have ironic effects. The charter's lofty statements defending principles of local self-determination imposed conditions on the West that, for the most part, Western nations did not intend to fulfill. In turn, that failure fueled an explosion of ethnic, nationalist, and religious anger at Western states, businesses, and institutions.

Mark A. Noll, *Books & Culture*, November/December 1998.

By the late 1960s, then, for idealists (the most notoriously unrelenting of whom are the young) there was much cause for cynicism. The euphoria of victory in the aftermath of World War II, which even affected the vanquished through programs such as the Marshall Plan and the reconstruction of Japan, evaporated in the wake of failed economic recoveries, subverted independence movements, and the Cold War stalemate. Within the dominant superpowers themselves and their client states, the capacity of the individual citizen to influence the course of events had seemingly shriveled to the vanishing point. Rather, political life appeared dominated by the remote, impersonal state and economic life by the multinational firm. Philosophers such as Herbert Marcuse and Jurgen Habermas described the resulting human dilemmas.

It is against this backdrop that we can understand the appeal of many of the social and political developments of the second half of the twentieth century. The civil rights and countercultural movements, the concern with environmentalism, perestroika, religious fundamentalism, and the recrudescence of ethnonationalism on a near planetary scale may all be interpreted as the search for a meaningful cause. It is even possible to regard the Yuppie movement as the reverse side of the same coin, in which the individual elevates a concern with self to the status of cause.

The nemesis, the ready foil that catalyzed such reactions, was the faceless, impersonal, and ultimately sinister forces represented by distant and insensitive elites protected by operatives identified by such acronyms as FBI, CIA, KGB. The central morality play informing twentieth-century artistic expression has been the individual's struggle within an alien world that is designed specifically to suppress self-expression. Whether described in Kafkaesque or Orwellian terms, painted by postexpressionists or portrayed by *Apocalypse Now*, the plot is essentially the same—individual survival within an alien environment.

Dropping out, affiliation with a social or religious movement, and fixation upon oneself are alternate ways of coping with the dilemmas of the late twentieth-century condition. Each is a means of humanizing a dehumanized world, at least in terms of one's own circumstances. Each has the potential of creating individuals so alienated that they become prone to antisocial violent behavior. In the cases of the pathological dropout and violent egomaniac there is the consensus that their violent acts are deranged behavior. Thus, as horrible as may be the wanton shootings of children in a California schoolyard, or John W. Hinckley Jr.'s attack on President Reagan in order to impress the actress Jodie Foster, each perpetrator was acting out a personal agenda whose implications for the rest of us (excluding the immediate victims) was but minimal. The same may not be said for persons prepared to employ violence in the name of a social or political cause. It is at this point that we are dealing with behavior that is often labeled "terrorist."

VARIATIONS ON TERRORISM

In this regard terrorism assumes several guises. There is the ecoterrorism of persons defending old-growth forests by driving spikes into trees in order to intimidate the sawmill workers who can be injured when processing them. There are the kidnappings and assassinations in defense of the working class by groups such as Italy's Brigata Rossa and Germany's Baader Meinhof activists. There are the Muslim fundamentalists in North Africa and parts of the Middle East employing violence in pursuit of sectarian goals. But by far the most salient form, the one that has demonstrated the greatest staying power to date, is the political violence of ethnonationalists, the self-styled guardians and avenging angels of ethnic homelands real and imagined. In Europe the two most prominent, though far from exclusive, examples would be the Irish Republican Army (IRA) and the Basques' ETA or Euzkadi ta Alkartasuna (Basque Country and Freedom).

In short, twentieth-century developments have created a climate favoring the resort to violence by a variety of politically alienated individuals and groups.

| "Democratic principles may actually encourage terrorist activity."

DEMOCRACY ENCOURAGES TERRORISM

David C. Rapoport

Nations ruled by democratic governments may be more likely to face acts of terrorism than other countries, argues David C. Rapoport in the following viewpoint. He asserts that democratic principles may motivate terrorism because the right to vote and the freedom of speech do not give individuals as much political power as they might expect. Rapoport contends that people who disagree with the majority rule might feel marginalized and respond with terrorism. Rapoport is a professor emeritus in the political science department at the University of California at Los Angeles and the joint editor of *Terrorism and Political Violence*, a journal.

As you read, consider the following questions:

1. Who were the first modern rebel terrorists, according to the author?
2. How much likelier is the development of terrorist groups in a democratic society, compared to a nondemocratic society, as cited by Rapoport?
3. According to Rapoport, what was John Stuart Mill's argument concerning multiethnic societies?

Reprinted from David C. Rapoport, "Fertile Ground for Terrorism," *San Diego Union-Tribune*, May 28, 1995, by permission of the author.

Democracies permit dissent and most Americans believe this means that terror is far less likely to appear in democratic states. The Oklahoma City horror has decimated this illusion. We foster this illusion partly because we pay so little attention to our own history where, in fact, the illusion appears frequently only to be shattered and revived again.

The Weather Underground and related groups, for example, initiated a wave of terror in the 1960s. The Anarchists and the Industrial Workers of the World, or Wobblies, thrived from the beginning of the 20th century to the 1920s. After the Civil War the Ku Klux Klan had its heyday. And no country in the past one hundred fifty years has had its head of state assassinated more often than we have.

DEMOCRACY ENCOURAGES TERRORISM

Our history gives us good reason to suspect that democratic principles may actually encourage terrorist activity, though the suspicion is rarely voiced today because democrats (can one be anything else now?) find it too uncomfortable to discuss.

Long ago, when democracy was examined more critically, many argued that no form of government produces more internal political violence. The Federalist Papers, an authoritative guide to the thought of the Founding Fathers, propounded this view.

So did Sir Henry Maine, a British legal historian, who observed that the spread of democracy in the 19th century was associated everywhere with more and more internal violence. These writers did not have terrorism in mind; but the issue they raised is fundamentally the same as that which the Oklahoma City horror poses.

EVIDENCE OF A CONNECTION

The historical connections between democracy and terror are suggestive. "Terror" and "terrorist" as political terms derive from the Reign of Terror, the purpose of which was to make France into the first European democracy. The first modern rebel terrorists, those who created the doctrine and strategy for contemporary terrorism emerged in late 19th century Russia announcing that their ultimate objective was to be a parliamentary democracy. Many anti-colonial uprisings around the world after World War II employed terrorism, and all claimed to be inspired by democratic ideals.

And there is other troubling evidence. In the *Journal of Terrorism and Political Violence*, Professors William Eubank and Leonard Weinberg of the University of Nevada-Reno, argue that evidence gathered in 172 sovereign states from 1954 to 1987 shows that terrorist groups are nearly four times as likely to develop in democratic than in non-democratic states.

Even more surprising, they found no significant difference between stable developed democracies and unstable or partially democratic ones!

THE REASONS FOR TERRORISM IN DEMOCRACIES

Why does democracy produce more than its share of terrorist groups? The conventional response is that terrorism flourishes when police powers are restricted and where there exists a sensation seeking media. But there is much more to the link between democracy and terror than that.

The expectations democracy creates are at the root of one set of causes. We are promised empowerment through the ballot but the vote doesn't really give the individual much power after all. Consequently, democracies often produce groups who feel themselves marginalized and willing to attack those deemed responsible for their condition.

FREEDOMS BEGET TERRORISM

Modern democracies have certain characteristics that make them extremely vulnerable to terrorist operations. . . . In democracies there is freedom of movement; people are free to come and go without the kind of surveillance that often exists in closed societies. Similarly, there is freedom of association; the state does not prevent like-minded individuals from forming private groups and organizations. Third, open societies furnish would-be terrorists with an abundance of targets to strike. The legal systems require the presentation of evidence, proof of guilt and various due process protections before someone can be imprisoned for participating in terrorist activities. . . . The relative ease with which potential terrorists are able to obtain weapons and transfer funds form one anonymously-held bank account to another [are] additional factors that contribute to the democracy-terrorism linkage.

William Lee Eubank and Leonard Weinberg, *Terrorism and Political Violence*, Winter 1994.

Free speech does not give one ability to be heard, and terror is often understood as communication which commands attention. The language of dissent may release passions we cannot control. Finally, when a system such as ours is born in a revolutionary upheaval, the precedent can inflame imaginations of future generations.

TREATMENT OF MINORITIES

Key democratic concepts produce another set of causes. The distinction we must make between the government and the source of its legitimacy, "the People," is potentially troublesome, and under certain circumstances leads some to believe that governmental claims to represent "the People" are not credible and that "the People" would support the rebels if the government allows true freedom.

Majority rule works well only when minorities consider themselves part of the same body politic. How prophetic was the 19th century philosopher John Stuart Mill's argument that tensions in a multiethnic society are generally (made worse) when democracy is introduced. In recent times, in many parts of the world ethnic violence and terror exploded when democratic principles were adopted.

Does this mean we are likely to have periods of terror so long as we remain democratic? Very likely. But we can take some comfort in recognizing that our experience is not new and that we have dealt successfully with the issues posed by terrorists before. Finally, although most stable democracies have been shaken by terror from time to time, terrorists have rarely toppled a democratic system.

"Growing poverty, desperation, and resentment ... provide a fertile recruiting ground to supply troops for the Osama bin Ladens of the world."

ECONOMIC DISTRESS MOTIVATES TERRORISTS

Allen Hammond

In the following viewpoint, Allen Hammond argues that economic problems around the globe could lead to an increase in terrorism. He contends that trends such as an increased income gap, environmental degradation, and overpopulation have created problems for developing countries that may encourage the growth of terrorist movements. Hammond asserts that addressing these problems is the proper approach to counterterrorism. Hammond is a senior scientist and director of strategic analysis at the World Resources Institute in Washington, D.C., an institution that seeks to foster environmentally sound development. He is the author of *WhichWorld? Scenarios for the 21st Century*.

As you read, consider the following questions:
1. Why are fisheries in trouble, according to Hammond?
2. According to statistics cited by the author, by how much will China's urban population increase by 2010?
3. What was sophisticated about the bombings in Kenya and Tanzania, in Hammond's opinion?

Reprinted from Allen Hammond, "Terrorism's Roots," *The Christian Science Monitor*, October 7, 1998, by permission of the author. This article was adapted from the author's book *WhichWorld? Scenarios for the Twenty-first Century* (Island Press, 1998).

President Clinton's plea for global action against terrorism and his effort to gear up US counterterrorism forces is a step in the right direction. But heightened preparedness and rapid response after an incident may do little to lessen the violence in the absence of policies that also address the root causes—growing poverty, desperation, and resentment. At the very least, such conditions provide a fertile recruiting ground to supply troops for the Osama bin Ladens of the world.

Might the tens of millions of Indonesians who suddenly find themselves plunged from growing prosperity back into poverty direct their resentment not just inward at the Chinese ethnic minority, but also outward at world capitalism? Antiterrorism programs will not redress their concerns nor help alleviate their suffering. Although Indonesia is a dramatic instance of such suffering, it isn't an isolated case.

THE RISE OF TROUBLED COUNTRIES

The number of countries in distress is likely to grow, if several trends continue:

Rising inequity. Not only is the gap between incomes in the industrial world and those in developing countries growing steadily wider, but so is awareness of the vast difference in lifestyle, thanks to the pervasiveness of television and growing international tourism. No wonder attempts at illegal immigration are rising, as is resentment among those who have abandoned hope of ever having the wealth, comfort, and opportunities they associate with the rich world.

Increasing environmental degradation and resource scarcity. Fisheries are in trouble virtually everywhere, as huge industrial trawlers overexploit a declining resource and coastal development destroys the wetlands, coral reefs, and other habitats critical to maintenance of breeding stocks. Yet it is the local fishermen in poor countries who are most likely to lose their livelihoods as a result, and the nearly 1 billion people for whom fish are the primary source of protein who are at risk of malnutrition. Rising demand for forest products, especially paper, threatens to devastate many of the world's remaining forests in coming decades—along with the way of life of the hundreds of thousands who depend on forests.

Rapidly growing populations in many parts of South Asia, Africa, and the Middle East mean that supplies of fertile land, pasture, firewood, and water are increasingly inadequate to meet the demand—driving some deeper into poverty and raising ethnic tensions. Such conditions in themselves do not necessarily lead to conflict and violence, but they provide ready tinder to catch a spark: It is not surprising that ethnic violence flared in Rwanda, since it has the highest population density and the most severe land scarcity in sub-Saharan Africa. And in the aftermath of that violence, resentment of the West, whether rational or not, is at an all-time high.

Rapid urbanization. Urban populations are increasing by 1 million a week, far faster than decent housing, water supplies, and other infrastructure can be built. In China alone, urban populations are expected to swell nearly 300 million by 2010.

WORRISOME QUESTIONS

As the urban explosion continues, it raises troubling questions for many developing countries. Will there be enough jobs in these burgeoning and increasingly polluted cities, or will urban poverty and squalor expand too? Will growing crime and massive unemployment pose a threat to social stability? And will these conditions encourage the rise of terrorist movements or schools for terrorists as they already have in the Palestinian refugee camps and the crowded slums of Pakistan?

INJUSTICE MOTIVATES TERRORISM

In many cases, the cause which the terrorist espouses is driven by a sense of injustice, as when a nation does not have independence in the family of nations, or where a minority feels that its rights are ignored. The world must ensure that no situations of political injustice continue, thereby removing this kind of terrorist's motivation, justification and support. Bahá'u'lláh [the founder of the Bahá'í Faith] emphasised the need for a universal conference at which the international frontiers will be fixed, and levels of national armaments reduced. Every minority would have its rights guaranteed.

Spiritual Assembly of the Bahá'ís of Warwick, "The Causes of Terrorism," found at http://www.fragrant.demon.co.uk/terror.html.

The attacks against US embassies in Kenya and Tanzania should be taken as a warning that the recruiting grounds for terrorists are expanding. Now Afghanistan and east Africa. Perhaps soon Indonesia, parts of southern Africa, and other parts of Africa. Perhaps Russia (if its collapse continues) and the Balkans. We may be entering a new era of violence, one characterized not just by a new level of ruthlessness but also by widespread availability of more dangerous technologies.

Information on how to build bombs and even more sophisticated weapons is widespread and impossible to control. US authorities in Washington and New York are preparing training exercises to prepare for the possibility of terrorist attacks with biological warfare agents. As the Russian economy crumbles, official concern over the integrity of that country's control over its nuclear weapons is rising rapidly.

Although the bombs used in Kenya and Tanzania were not sophisticated, the timing and coordination of the cellular phone-based network that planned the attacks was. With cellular-phone networks and the ability to encrypt Internet messages expanding rapidly, both terrorists and global criminal organizations have new and hard-to-trace ways to move information and money. Access to the means for violence, in short, is growing.

ADDRESSING THE MOTIVATIONS

Such an assessment does not mean that counterterrorism efforts are futile. But interception is inherently difficult and will get more so, and the ability to catch the terrorists afterward won't stop the violence from happening. All the more reason to try to reduce the motivation for violence, to address the underlying causes of terrorism. But so far, we have not been willing to make the effort, nor do the new Clinton proposals get us there.

> "Suicide terrorism has been allowed by Hamas leaders as a measure of tactical revenge for humiliating Israeli actions."

ISRAELI ACTIONS MOTIVATE MIDDLE EAST TERRORISTS

Ehud Sprinzak

In the following viewpoint, Ehud Sprinzak argues that revenge against humiliating Israeli policies is what motivates the Palestinian organization Hamas to commit acts of terrorism. Sprinzak contends that, contrary to the view of Israeli leaders, Hamas does not seek to destroy the Israeli government. He asserts that Hamas' terrorism is instead in response to Israeli actions such as increased West Bank settlements and the assassination of a Hamas leader. Sprinzak is a professor of political science at Hebrew University in Jerusalem and the author of *Brother Against Brother: Violence and Extremism in Israeli Politics from Altalena to the Rabin Assassination.*

As you read, consider the following questions:

1. What event prompted Hamas to begin suicide bombings within Israel, according to the author?
2. In Sprinzak's view, why is Hamas popular among ordinary Palestinians?
3. According to the author, what changes could lessen Hamas' motivations for terrorism?

Reprinted from Ehud Sprinzak, "Learning to Live with Hamas," *The Washington Post National Weekly Edition*, October 27, 1997, by permission of the author.

In an interview on "60 Minutes," Hassan Salameh, arch terrorist of the Palestinian group Hamas, confirmed what had been long suspected by students of the Mideast conflict: that the assassination of Yehiya Ayash, a Hamas leader known as "the Engineer," had prompted his followers to organize the three suicide bombings that stunned Israel in 1996. Salameh said that he smuggled explosives into Israel a day after the funeral of Ayash, who had masterminded the suicide bombings that terrorized Israel from April 1994 to the summer of 1995. Ayash was killed by an exploding cellular phone planted by Israeli agents.

DIFFERENT THEORIES FOR HAMAS TERRORISM

Salameh's statement suggests that the 1996 suicide bombings did not stem from a strategic decision to bring down the Israeli peace government, as former Labor Party prime minister Shimon Peres and others have contended. Rather, it was triggered by a desire to avenge Ayash's death.

It is not difficult to guess why Israeli authorities (who must have heard Salameh's claim when they interrogated him months ago) would have little interest in sharing this sort of information with the public. In 1996, Peres experienced a dramatic decline in popularity because of the Hamas bombings. He could not admit that his risky order to execute the Engineer had precipitated the return of suicide terrorism. It was more expedient to tell Israelis that Hamas wished to bring his government down.

Peres's successor, Binyamin Netanyahu, also needs to demonize Hamas. He does not truly believe in the Oslo peace process, never has. Citing the public rhetoric of Hamas—which since 1988 has called for the destruction of Israel—helps him make his case.

HAMAS SEEKS REVENGE

This dissection of the motivation for Hamas terrorism may seem talmudic to some, but it is important. The history of Hamas—in contrast to its stereotypical image in the Western media—suggests that its opposition to the peace process has never led Hamas leaders to adopt a strategy of wholesale suicide bombing. Rather, suicide terrorism has been allowed by Hamas leaders as a measure of tactical revenge for humiliating Israeli actions.

This history is especially relevant in the wake of Israel's foiled assassination plot against a Hamas leader in Jordan. When Palestinian bodyguards captured the two would-be assassins, Jordan's King Hussein forced Israel to release Sheik Ahmed Yassin, the blind cleric who founded Hamas in 1987. Yassin's return to a hero's welcome in Gaza raised fears in Israel and Washington that Palestinian terrorism had been strengthened.

In fact, the evolution of Hamas and its policy of armed struggle against Israel suggests that Sheik Yassin may prove to be a moderating influence.

During the *intifada*, the Palestinian uprisings that shook the Israeli-occupied territories from 1987 to 1993, Hamas increasingly attacked Israeli soldiers and settlers, citing the right of self-defense against illegal foreign occupation. The organization, however, showed no intention of blowing up buses carrying innocent civilians inside Israel.

Hamas resorted to this atrocious type of terrorism only after February 1994 when Baruch Goldstein, an Israeli physician and army reserve captain, massacred 29 praying Palestinians in a Hebron shrine. Hamas vowed to teach Israelis a lesson they would never forget. The pledge was to put the Jews through a number of infernos of the kind experienced by the Hebronites. Joined by members of a smaller group, Islamic Jihad, Hamas terrorists mounted seven suicide bombings within Israel proper.

STOPPING AND STARTING HAMAS TERRORISM

This series of suicide strikes—and Israeli counter strikes—exhausted itself in the summer of 1995. The assassination of prime minister Yitzhak Rabin in November 1995 probably provided an added sobering effect on both the Hamas leadership and Israeli security officials.

At that point, the Palestinians had little reason to complain. The Peres government had overseen a large Israeli redeployment from West Bank cities that produced many smiling faces in Gaza and the West Bank. There was little doubt of Peres's personal commitment to peace, and tens of thousands of Palestinian workers brought their bread from Israel. Hamas, including its extremist wing abroad, showed little interest in resuming suicide bombings and even allowed the semi-retirement of the Engineer in a remote Gaza strip town. Without Ayash's execution, it is quite likely that Israel would not have experienced the three suicide bombings in 1996 that killed 55 people and wounded 265. The recent wave of Hamas suicide bombings, the third in the series, did not start after the 1996 ascendance of Netanyahu to power. Nor did it follow the Jerusalem tourist tunnel fiasco on September 1996, which led to rioting, gunfire exchanges between Palestinian and Israeli policemen and the deaths of more than 80 people.

What restarted the Hamas suicide bombing machine was a

series of Israeli insults since the beginning of 1997: Netanyahu's calculated decision to humiliate the Palestinians by building in the Jerusalem neighborhood of Har Homa, by effectively ending agreed-upon redeployment of troops from the occupied territories, by cynically insulting Yasser Arafat and by resuming West Bank settlement on a large scale.

A Simplistic View of Hamas

The view that Hamas is an organization that will resort to terrorism anywhere, anytime is simplistic. Why, for example, did Hamas leaders not resort to suicide bombings before April 1994; between August 1995 and February 1996; and between March 1996 and July 1997?

The official Israeli explanation (which presupposes the existence of a grand Hamas strategy of suicide terrorism) gives much credit to the Israeli secret services and a small amount to the cooperation of Arafat's security forces. Though not entirely false, this theory has serious flaws.

The militants of Hamas, if they are willing to take great risk, can mount operations that escape detection by the Israeli and Palestinian authorities. There are huge amounts of explosives in the West Bank and Gaza. There are sophisticated "graduates" of Israeli prisons, such as Salameh, ready to organize terror strikes. And there are dozens of young Palestinians ready to die, if only asked.

Islam Is Not the Threat

The stepped-up pressure by the Palestinian Authority and Israel on Islamic militants has followed the media's invention of a myth that Islam breeds violence, which only plays into the hands of militant groups that claim to represent Islam. . . .

In fact, the real challenge to peace lies not in radical Islam but in everyday reality. Muslims (and Christians) on the West Bank live under an occupation, with its daily humiliations, expropriations and violence.

Azmi Bishara, *New York Times*, February 17, 1995.

A better explanation for Hamas's willingness to refrain from violence is found in the nature of the Hamas movement. In contrast to its most persistent image in the Western media, Hamas is not just a terrorist group comprised of criminal suicide bombers in the occupied territories and a radical faction in Damascus that orders bloody operations against innocent civilians.

It also is a large socio-religious movement involved in communal work within Palestinian refugee camps. It is responsible for the building and maintenance of hundreds of mosques and religious schools, dozens of clinics, nurseries, and adult education centers. Its origins go back to the largely nonviolent Muslim Brotherhood, which started in Palestine in the 1940s.

The reason Hamas is so popular among ordinary Palestinians (an estimated 20 percent to 30 percent describe themselves as supporters), is not because the group has killed and wounded hundreds of Israelis, but because the organization has made it possible for hundreds of thousands of Palestinians to survive and live a semblance of a decent life. In contrast with many Palestine Liberation Organization (PLO) activists around Arafat who have become increasingly corrupt, the Hamas activists are honest. That the majority of them live among the poor only increases their appeal.

THE GROWTH OF ARMED STRUGGLE

The Muslim Brotherhood was not always supportive of armed struggle against Israel. In 1979, the Israeli government tacitly supported the establishment of an affiliated political organization, the Muslim Association, in an effort to draw support away from Arafat's PLO. The group took up arms only in 1988. After years of nonviolent educational and communal work, it was not an easy decision for the group. It met resistance from a number of clerics who were afraid that terrorism and life in the underground would destroy their daily contacts with the people. But the brutal reality of the Israeli repression during the intifada and the pressure of more radical groups led Sheik Yassin and others to establish Hamas as a political and military organization.

Neither Yassin nor other Hamas has ever given up the movement's legal infrastructure and its charitable work. Though terrorism against settlers and soldiers has become an increasingly popular response to Israel's massive arrests, violence was never allowed to become the main occupation of the organization. The vast majority of Hamas operatives, though hostile to the Oslo process and critical of the PLO, have, nevertheless, continued to work with the poor and remained committed to the construction of a Palestinian civil society. Yassin, upon his release from prison, reiterated the group's position that Arafat is the only legitimate leader of the Palestinians and that Hamas would act against him only as a loyal opposition.

It goes without saying that the life of the Israelis and the implementation of the Oslo accords would have been much easier without the terrorism of Hamas's military wing. But the complex motivations of Hamas leaders suggest that this Muslim organization is not the insurmountable obstacle to peace that most Americans (and Israelis) believe it to be.

Three conclusions deserve particular attention.

• Whether we like it or not, Hamas is a Palestinian fact of life. Those who demand the elimination of this organization as a pre-condition for peace are saying, in effect, that there will never be peace.

• Aggressive policies by the government of Israel such as a unilateral continuation of settlements and the assassination of Hamas leaders are bound to drive the organization's heads to resume suicide bombings inside Israel.

• The continued presence of Hamas on the Palestinian scene does not imply perennial suicide bombing. It is, in fact, likely that a significant improvement in the political and socio-economic conditions of the Palestinian masses—and their recognition that terrorism and instability threaten these achievements—will reduce Hamas's incentives to commit atrocities against Israeli civilians and drive its pragmatic leaders to greater cooperation with the Palestinian Authority.

"In virtually every one of his speeches
to the Palestinian multitudes,
[Yasir] Arafat . . . invariably urges
jihad against Israel."

PALESTINIAN LEADERS MOTIVATE
MIDDLE EAST TERRORISTS

David Bar-Illan

In the following viewpoint, David Bar-Illan contends that the
policies and rhetoric of the Palestinian Liberation Organization,
particularly its leader Yasir Arafat, motivate Middle East terrorists
such as Hamas. Bar-Illan maintains that Arafat's actions, such as
sheltering terrorists and lionizing martyred terrorists in speeches,
encourages further violence against Israel. However, he asserts,
these actions and misleading statements by Arafat have been over-
looked by Israel's government (then led by Shimon Peres) and
the Clinton administration. Bar-Illan is a senior advisor for Israeli
prime minister Benjamin Netanyahu.

As you read, consider the following questions:

1. According to Bar-Illan, how is Arafat different from other
   sponsors of terrorism?
2. What group did Arafat blame for the February 1996 bus
   bombings, according to the author?
3. In Bar-Illan's opinion, what did the March 1996 State
   Department report on the Oslo accords ignore?

Excerpted from David Bar-Illan, "The Wages of Oslo," Commentary, May 1996. Reprinted
by permission; all rights reserved.

What Western interpreters have consistently obscured is that Hamas and Islamic Jihad do not, in fact, oppose the Oslo process [peace talks between Israel and the Palestine Liberation Organization (PLO), highlighted by the September 1993 signing of a peace agreement]. Although they object to any final settlement that would entail Arab recognition of Israel's legitimacy, they most emphatically favor Israeli withdrawal from "occupied territories," as dictated by the Oslo accords. Nor have they ever raised a hand against the PLO, the co-signatory of Oslo and an organization to which the Hamas charter refers as "father, brother, mentor, and close relative." Hamas may regard itself as [Palestinian leader Yasir] Arafat's political competitor—it would like to rule an Islamic Palestine—but at this particular stage the two are following the traditional shoot-and-talk strategy of all dictatorships negotiating with democratic adversaries.

That strategy, rooted not only in doctrine but experience, has been all too effective. As Yossi Klein Halevi, a senior writer for the *Jerusalem Report* (and initially an enthusiastic supporter of the Oslo agreements), put it in a *New York Times* article:

> At this stage of Palestinian nation-building, terrorism can be useful. The existence of a radical alternative strengthens Arafat's international legitimacy as a moderate leader and adds urgency to his demands for additional financing for the Palestinian Authority. Indeed, it was the growing power of Hamas that initially persuaded a skeptical Prime Minister Yitzhak Rabin to accept the PLO as a negotiating partner. Terrorism is also a psychological weapon, which helps ensure continued Israeli territorial concessions. Each new terrorist attack increases the number of Israelis demanding total separation from the Palestinians. The political consequence of that emotional response is greater Israeli acceptance of a Palestinian state. Thus, while Arafat may on occasion respond to international pressure and crack down on terrorism, he won't uproot the large-scale Hamas infrastructure that has grown in Gaza, at least for now.

ARAFAT SPONSORS TERRORISM

It is, then, ludicrous to accuse Arafat of not having done enough to curb terrorism, as both [then-Israeli Prime Minister Shimon] Peres and U.S. Secretary of State Warren Christopher did in the aftermath of the latest bombings. No leader in the world better fits the description, "sponsor of terrorism," than he. Not only does he shelter terrorists; he lets them incite, recruit, organize, train, arm, raise funds, and launch operations from areas under his control. Even Peres finally admitted in mid-March 1996 that "the head of the snake is in Gaza," the area under Arafat's primary command.

It was the Hamas leadership in Arafat's Gaza, keeping on cordial terms with his Palestinian Authority, which decided on terrorist strikes and issued operational orders for the bus bombings. It was Arafat's Gaza where the Hamas military organization trained bombers and assembled explosives, where "The Engineer," the mastermind of suicide bombings which killed 50 Israelis, found shelter and PLO protection, and where his successor, Mohammed Dief, was living openly. In fact, Arafat's chief of preventive security was negotiating with Dief—a close friend—both before and after the first bus bombing in Jerusalem. Knowing of Dief's involvement in the bombing, he did nothing either to detain him or to prevent the next outrage.

Nor, unlike Hafez Assad of Syria and other international sponsors of terrorism, does Arafat bother to keep a safe distance from the killers in order to preserve "deniability." Arafat himself elevated Ayyash to sainthood, paying a condolence call on Hamas leaders after his death, lauding him as a martyr and hero, and arranging for the Palestinian police to participate in the funeral and fire a 21-gun salute in the terrorist's honor. It was with Arafat's knowledge and approval that commemorations for Ayyash were held throughout the West Bank and Gaza, including one in Kalkilya three days before the first Jerusalem attack in which a crude mock-up of an Israeli bus marked (after an earlier successful terrorist assault) "Dizengoff 5" in Hebrew was burned in the town square.

Arafat participates—usually through an amplified telephone—in Hamas rallies like the one held in 1995 at the Abu Dis Islamic campus in Jerusalem. There the main speaker, Sheikh Jamil Hamami, intoned:

> We have not forgotten for a single day Jerusalem, Haifa Jaffa . . .
> and all of Palestine. The road is very long, but you must continue
> on it until victory or death for Allah. My wish is to die a martyr.

Hamami was later tried by an Israeli court; the PLO paid for his legal defense.

INCITING TERRORISM

In virtually every one of his speeches to the Palestinian multitudes, Arafat demands the release from Israeli prison of Sheikh Ahmad Yassin, Hamas founder and spiritual leader, and he invariably urges jihad against Israel. Although he has assured Peres and the Western media that jihad means "nonviolent improvement" or even a "love letter," he always accompanies the call with exhortations to sacrifice, death, and martyrdom; alludes to the precedent whereby the Prophet Muhammad signed treaties with enemies when his own following was weak, only to scuttle them and emerge triumphant when he became stronger; lionizes and glorifies terrorists who have died in the struggle against Israel, including those who have attacked Israelis *after* the signing of the Oslo accords; and refers repeatedly to the PLO's 1974 "plan of stages" for Israel's destruction. After terrorist incidents in Israel, Arafat has invariably freed the Hamas operatives who had been just as routinely rounded up by the Palestinian police.

A SANCTUARY FOR TERRORISTS

Oslo—shorthand for the historic agreement signed on the South Lawn of the White House by Yitzhak Rabin and Yasir Arafat [in September 1993]—sanctioned the Palestine Liberation Organization (PLO) as a legitimate negotiating partner for Israel and sanctioned the eventual emergence of an independent Palestinian "entity."

It did not sanction a Palestinian sanctuary—on land painfully given up by Israel—for terrorists.

Yet this is what we have now in the Gaza Strip and those areas of the West Bank under the control of the Palestinian Authority.

The B'nai B'rith Center for Public Policy, "Palestinian Terrorism: Crime Without Punishment," February 1998.

But—say Arafat's apologists—there is no denying that Fatah, his own organization in the PLO, has eschewed terrorism, and that at least two-thirds of the Palestinian population have decided to lay down their arms. This, too, is misleading. True, since the signing of the Oslo agreement Arafat's Fatah organization and his bodyguards in Force 17 have not (with a few exceptions) attacked Jews. But for a clearer indication of the PLO's disposition we have not only Arafat's own words quoted above, but the pronouncements of his closest lieutenants.

Thus, Nabil Shaath, the PA's Minister of Planning and a favorite Arafat negotiator, said in a Nablus symposium (telecast on local Palestinian television):

If the negotiations reach a dead end, we shall go back to the struggle and strife, as we did for 40 years. It is not beyond our capabilities. . . . As long as Israel goes forward [with the process], there are no problems, which is why we observe the agreements of peace and nonviolence. But if and when Israel will say, "That's it, we won't talk about Jerusalem, we won't return refugees, we won't dismantle settlements and we won't retreat from borders," then all the acts of violence will return. Except that this time we'll have 30,000 armed Palestinian soldiers who will operate in areas in which we have unprecedented elements of freedom.

As if to complement these statements, another Arafat spokesman, Marwan Bargouti, told the (London) *Independent* that Palestinian security forces have been ordered to fire if Israeli soldiers ever try to enter territories under the PA's control. He added that the Palestinians are in possession of many more weapons than the agreement allows, and that their armed forces are much larger than advertised. Still another Fatah spokesman, according to the Washington Institute for Near East Policy, "warned London's *Sharq al-Awsat* newspaper [in mid-March 1996] . . . that violence and terrorism against Israel [would] be expected until Israel withdraws fully from the territories."

ARAFAT REPEATS LIES

An interesting insight into Arafat's mind is afforded by his habit of charging that *Israeli* "extremists" were complicit in 1996's bus bombings. "Only a superman would have been capable of executing such a complicated operation without Israeli help," Arafat told one visitor, and then proceeded to name the purported Israeli organization involved: the OAS, after the clandestine right-wing group in the French army which in the late 1950's opposed French withdrawal from Algeria. Nor was this the first time he had made such a charge. Following the Beit Lid bombing in January 1995, which killed 22 Israelis, and again after the bus bombing in Jerusalem of August 1995, in which four Israelis died, he said similar things, and at one time even identified Ehud Barak, then chief of the General Staff and now Israel's Foreign Minister, as a leader of the group.

Of course it is doubtful that Arafat really believes in the existence of an Israeli OAS, any more than he believes Israel's ten-agora coin contains a secret map of expansion; that the blue stripes on Israel's flag represent the Nile and Euphrates rivers, the promised borders of "Greater Israel" in the Bible; or for that matter that Jesus was a Palestinian Arab—all things he has repeatedly avowed. Rather, he must assume that such lies—no matter how outrageous—will stick if repeated often enough. He is not the first dictator in history to assume so, and to be proved right. At the very least, Arafat clearly hopes to implant in Western minds a suspicion that those responsible for the bombings were not members of an Islamic organization with which he himself has repeatedly professed close relations and solidarity.

By floating these lies, moreover, Arafat risks nothing. Diplomats and journalists who hear his earnest descriptions of conspiracy may relate the story to their colleagues with an air of amused disbelief, but no one has ever called him to task for retailing such libelous fantasies, nor has doing so diminished the respect in which world leaders seem to hold him, or their resolve to help him with grants and loans. Even Yitzhak Rabin, who once stalked out of the room when Arafat attempted to sell him a similar canard, returned to continue negotiating.

Indeed, no matter how damning any of the evidence against Arafat, before February 25 of 1996 neither the government of Israel nor the Clinton administration ever found serious fault with his performance. The March 1, 1996, State Department report on compliance with the Oslo accords—required by law before additional aid could be approved—simply ignores the fact that the PLO has consistently violated virtually every aspect of the agreements and in particular has refused to extradite terrorists. Even after the February-March bombings, Secretary of State Christopher waited less than 48 hours after the routine round-ups began to state that Arafat was "doing 100 percent." For their part, Israeli officials have gone so far as to declare that anyone opposing American help for the PLO is no friend of Israel.

PROBLEMS IN GAZA

Nor, finally, is it only Arafat's support for violence against Israel which both the Israeli government and the U.S. administration have chosen to overlook. Although virtually every official report from Gaza has paid glowing tribute to the supposedly "wonderful improvements" wrought by the PA, a rather different picture emerges from a harrowing story filed in the Hebrew daily Ha'aretz by Gideon Levy, a former assistant to Peres and an ardent advocate of a Palestinian state.

Levy was brought to a Gaza apartment in December 1995 to hear testimonies by victims of the new regime. The window shutters were tightly closed, and Levy's host and his host's mother kept nervously checking the street for unusual movement. Everyone spoke in whispers for fear the neighbors might hear. Although the tales varied in detail, they were uniform in essence:

> For many hours they told stories of bribery, exploitation, extortion, incarceration without trial, drug dealings, car thefts, prostitution, and everything imaginable.

> A father says he has no idea what his son is being accused of. "It's not only my son, it's the whole nation," he says. "The security people said they were taking him for five minutes; seven months have passed since then. In my life I have seen the Turks,

the British, the Egyptians, and the Israelis. But I have never experienced this kind of situation. . . ."

An embittered woman says, "I have come to you from under the earth. My husband does not know I am here. He was told that he and his whole family would be liquidated if he reveals anything: We are endangered people now. . . . That's the face of the PA and that's what's come of it. We were happy, thinking we were being liberated from the occupation. Now God should chop off our hands which threw stones at the Jews. We brought this disaster on ourselves. Now there is no law and no justice."

Such testimonies are almost identical to those heard by numerous Israeli and foreign journalists in southern Lebanon in the wake of the Israeli invasion of 1982. There, too, the PLO had established a ministate, known in Israel as Fatahland. It was a state which an earlier generation of credulous Arafat groupies had praised for its hospitals and schools, its network of beneficent social institutions. In reality, it proved to be as savage and as corrupt as any Arab dictatorship in the Middle East.

Before assuming power in Gaza, Arafat boasted to skeptics that the PLO would run it expertly. "We acquired our experience," he said, "in Lebanon." So they did.

| "Terrorists tend to project their own antisocial motivations onto others, creating a polarized 'we versus they' outlook."

A COMBINATION OF FACTORS MOTIVATES TERRORISTS

Terrorism Research Center

In the following viewpoint, the Terrorism Research Center asserts that three types of motivation exist for terrorism: rational, psychological, and cultural. The center argues that each type of terrorist has different reasons for considering the use of violence, including the need to maintain group legitimacy and the fear of cultural extermination. The center contends that religion is the most dangerous of the cultural motivations for terrorism and is the source for some of the most violent incidents. The Terrorism Research Center is an independent institute that researches and analyzes terrorism, information warfare and other issues relating to political violence.

As you read, consider the following questions:

1. How do rational terrorists use cost-benefit analysis, according to the center?
2. In the center's view, why are terrorist groups prone to fracturing?
3. How does the violence in the United States differ from that in France or Germany, according to the center?

Reprinted from *The Basics of Terrorism*, Part 2: "The Terrorists," by the Terrorism Research Center, www.terrorism.com/terrorism/bpart2.html, by permission of the center.

Terrorists are inspired by many different motives. Students of terrorism classify them into three categories: rational, psychological, and cultural. A terrorist may be shaped by combinations of these.

RATIONAL MOTIVATION

The rational terrorist thinks through his goals and options, making a cost-benefit analysis. He seeks to determine whether there are less costly and more effective ways to achieve his objective than terrorism. To assess the risk, he weighs the target's defensive capabilities against his own capabilities to attack. He measures his group's capabilities to sustain the effort. The essential question is whether terrorism will work for the desired purpose, given societal conditions at the time. The terrorist's rational analysis is similar to that of a military commander or a business entrepreneur considering available courses of action.

Groups considering terrorism as an option ask a crucial question: Can terrorism induce enough anxiety to attain its goals without causing a backlash that will destroy the cause and perhaps the terrorists themselves? To misjudge the answer is to risk disaster. Recent history offers examples of several groups that had apparently good prospects for success which paid the price of misjudging reaction to terrorism. In the early 1970s, the Tupamaros in Uruguay and the ERP (People's Revolutionary Army) and Montoneros in Argentina misjudged a hostile popular reaction to terrorism. They pushed the societies beyond their threshold of tolerance and were destroyed as a result. The same is true of several groups operating in Turkey in the late 1970s and, possibly, several Mafiosi families in Italy in the 1990s.

PSYCHOLOGICAL MOTIVATION

Psychological motivation for terrorism derives from the terrorist's personal dissatisfaction with his life and accomplishments. He finds his raison d'etre in dedicated terrorist action. Although no clear psychopathy is found among terrorists, there is a nearly universal element in them that can be described as the "true believer." Terrorists do not even consider that they may be wrong and that others' views may have some merit. Terrorists tend to project their own antisocial motivations onto others, creating a polarized "we versus they" outlook. They attribute only evil motives to anyone outside their own group. This enables the terrorists to dehumanize their victims and removes any sense of ambiguity from their minds. The resulting clarity of purpose appeals to those who crave violence to relieve their constant anger. The other common characteristic of the psychologically motivated terrorist is the pronounced need to belong to a group. With some terrorists, group acceptance is a stronger motivator than the stated political objectives of the organization. Such individuals define their social status by group acceptance.

Terrorist groups with strong internal motivations find it necessary to justify the group's existence continuously. A terrorist group must terrorize. As a minimum, it must commit violent acts to maintain group self-esteem and legitimacy. Thus, terrorists sometimes carry out attacks that are objectively nonproductive or even counterproductive to their announced goal.

Another result of psychological motivation is the intensity of group dynamics among terrorists. They tend to demand unanimity and be intolerant of dissent. With the enemy clearly identified and unequivocally evil, pressure to escalate the frequency and intensity of operations is ever present. The need to belong to the group discourages resignations, and the fear of compromise disallows their acceptance. Compromise is rejected, and terrorist groups lean toward maximalist positions. Having placed themselves beyond the pale, forever unacceptable to ordinary society, they cannot accept compromise. They consider negotiation dishonorable, if not treasonous. This may explain why terrorist groups are prone to fracturing and why the splinters are frequently more violent than their parent group.

The Jewish experience in Palestine is a classic example of splintering. In 1931, Haganah B broke from Haganah; in 1936, Irgun Svai Leumi split from Haganah B; and in 1940, Lochamei Herut Israel, or the Stern Gang, broke from Irgun. Each successive group was more rigid and violence-prone than its parent.

The psychodynamics also make the announced group goal nearly impossible to achieve. A group that achieves its stated purpose is no longer needed; thus, success threatens the psychological well-being of its members. When a terrorist group approaches its stated goal, it is inclined to redefine it. The group may reject the achievement as false or inadequate or the result of the duplicity of "them." Nicaragua's Recontras, The Basque ETA (Euskadi Ta Askatasuna, "Basque Fatherland and Liberty"), and many Palestinian radical groups apparently suffer from fear of success. One effective psychological defense against success is to define goals so broadly that they are impossible to achieve. Even if the world proclaims the success of a political movement, the terrorists can deny it and fight on.

Cultural Motivation

Cultures shape values and motivate people to actions that seem unreasonable to foreign observers. Americans are reluctant to appreciate the intense effect of culture on behavior. We accept the myth that rational behavior guides all human actions. Even though irrational behavior occurs in our own tradition, we seek to explain it by other means. We reject as unbelievable such things as vendettas, martyrdom, and self-destructive group behavior when we observe them in others. We view with disbelief such things as the dissolution of a viable state for the sake of ethnic purity when the resulting ministates are economically anemic.

The treatment of life in general and individual life in particular is a cultural characteristic that has a tremendous impact on terrorism. In societies in which people identify themselves in terms of group membership (family, clan, tribe), there may be a willingness to self-sacrifice seldom seen elsewhere. (Note, however, that American soldiers are less surprised at heroic sacrifice for one's military unit; the difference among cultures is in the group with which one identifies.) At times, terrorists seem to be eager to give their lives for their organization and cause. The lives of "others," being wholly evil in the terrorists' value system, can be destroyed with little or no remorse.

Other factors include the manner in which aggression is channeled and the concepts of social organization. For example, the ambient level of violence is shaped by the political structure and its provisions for power transfer. Some political systems have no effective nonviolent means for the succession to power. A culture may have a high tolerance for nonpolitical violence, such as banditry or ethnic "turf" battles, and remain relatively free of political violence. The United States, for example, is one of the most violent societies in the world. Yet, political violence remains an aberration. By contrast, France and Germany, with low tolerance for violent crime, have a history of political violence.

FEARING THE VALUES OF OTHERS

A major cultural determinant of terrorism is the perception of "outsiders" and anticipation of a threat to ethnic group survival. Fear of cultural extermination leads to violence which, to someone who does not experience it, seems irrational. All human beings are sensitive to threats to the values by which they identify themselves. These include language, religion, group membership, and homeland or native territory. The possibility of losing any of these can trigger defensive, even xenophobic, reactions.

Religion may be the most volatile of cultural identifiers because it encompasses values deeply held. A threat to one's religion puts not only the present at risk but also one's cultural past and the future. Many religions, including Christianity and Islam, are so confident they are right that they have used force to obtain converts. Terrorism in the name of religion can be especially violent. Like all terrorists, those who are religiously motivated view their acts with moral certainty and even divine sanctions. What would otherwise be extraordinary acts of desperation become a religious duty in the mind of the religiously motivated terrorist. This helps explain the high level of commitment and willingness to risk death among religious extremist groups.

Periodical Bibliography

The following articles have been selected to supplement the diverse views presented in this chapter. Addresses are provided for periodicals not indexed in the *Readers' Guide to Periodical Literature*, the *Alternative Press Index*, the *Social Sciences Index*, or the *Index to Legal Periodicals and Books*.

Robert Bowman — "Truth Is, We're Terrorized Because We're Hated," *National Catholic Reporter*, October 2, 1998. Available from 115 E. Armour Blvd., Kansas City, MO 64111.

James Brooke — "Volatile Mixture in Viper Militia: Hatred Plus a Love for Guns," *New York Times*, July 5, 1996.

Caleb Carr — "Terrorism as Warfare: The Lessons of Military History," *World Policy Journal*, Winter 1996–1997.

Gus Constantine — "America's Image Explodes," *World & I*, August 1995. Available from 3600 New York Ave. NE, Washington, DC 20002.

Kevin Fedarko — "Who Wishes Us Ill?" *Time*, July 29, 1996.

Thomas L. Friedman — "Motives for the Bombing," *New York Times*, August 8, 1998.

William Norman Grigg — "No Enemies on the Left," *New American*, May 13, 1996. Available from American Opinion Publishing, Inc., 770 Westhill Blvd., Appleton, WI 54914.

David Hoffman — "On a One-Way Trip to Paradise," *Washington Post National Weekly Edition*, March 18–24, 1996. Available from Reprints, 1150 15th St. NW, Washington, DC 20071.

Nation — "The 'War of the Future,'" September 21, 1998.

David Nyhan — "Terrorists Share Similarities," *Liberal Opinion Week*, May 22, 1995. Available from PO Box 880, Vinton, IA 52349-0880.

Virginia I. Postrel — "Fighting Words," *Reason*, July 1995.

Tony Snow — "U.S. Foreign Policy Encourages Troublemakers," *Conservative Chronicle*, March 20, 1996. Available from PO Box 29, Hampton, IA 50441.

Ronald Steel — "When Worlds Collide," *New York Times*, July 21, 1996.

Evan Thomas — "Blood Brothers," *Newsweek*, April 22, 1996.

Rodney C. Watkins — "Making Sense of Terrorism," *Peace Review*, vol. 7, no. 3/4, 1995.

Stephen Zunes — "Terrorism by Another Name," *Peace Review*, vol. 7, no. 3/4, 1995.

CHAPTER 3

CAN TERRORISM BE JUSTIFIED?

CHAPTER PREFACE

The term terrorism originated over two hundred years ago, during the French Revolution—more specifically, the 1793–1794 Reign of Terror. Unlike modern terrorism, which is often associated with individuals or groups attacking a foreign or domestic government, the Reign of Terror was led by Maximilien Robespierre and other leaders of France's own government. Robespierre and the others who led the Committee of Public Safety (the group that was created in April 1793 to rule France) directed their violence toward people whom they believed posed threats to liberty. These perceived enemies—in particular, those who supported a different form of government, including a return to the monarchy—were arrested and often guillotined. The violence ended with the overthrow and execution of Robespierre. The actions and motivations of those responsible for the Reign of Terror are different from the causes championed by today's terrorists, but like their modern counterparts, faced with inciting violence and invariably causing death, Robespierre and his cohorts sought to justify their violence.

Terrorists often try to explain their philosophy, in order to give validity to their actions. In the view of Robespierre, violence by the government against potentially dangerous groups was necessary in order to protect liberty and quell tyranny. He said in a February 1794 speech: "Subdue by terror the enemies of liberty, and you will be right, as founders of the Republic. The government of the revolution is liberty's despotism against tyranny." The violence he endorsed became widespread, as twenty thousand people of various social classes and political views were executed over the course of the year.

Many people have repudiated Robespierre's justification. One of the most famous was Frederic Bastiat, a 19th-century French philosopher. In his 1850 pamphlet, The Law, Bastiat decries the Reign of Terror, arguing, "[Robespierre] wants a dictatorship in order that he may use terror to force upon the country his own principles of morality." According to Bastiat, Robespierre was arrogant to believe that he could change the values of mankind through the use of violence.

The justifications for modern-day terrorism often turn Robespierre's idea on its head, asserting that violence is needed to protect and liberate citizens from an allegedly tyrannical government. However, like Robespierre, today's terrorists often find their arguments dismissed and contradicted. In the following chapter, the contributors consider whether terrorism can be justified.

"Once you choose freedom, your only
choices will be either to knuckle
under for the moment or fight."

RESISTANCE TO TYRANNY JUSTIFIES VIOLENCE AGAINST THE U.S. GOVERNMENT

Martin Lindstedt

In the following viewpoint, Martin Lindstedt argues that violence against the U.S. government is justified because the government has ceased to be a democracy. According to Lindstedt, the government violates the Constitution and the rights of American citizens through tactics such as excessive taxation, unlawful imprisonment, and murder. He asserts that the present-day situation is worse than that faced by the colonies during the American Revolution and that the time has come to fight in order to create a better future. Lindstedt belongs to the 7th Missouri Militia and has edited several newsletters, including *Southwestern Missouri Libertarian*.

As you read, consider the following questions:

1. According to Lindstedt, when does a person have the right to revolution?
2. What percentage of colonists' income was taxed, according to the author?
3. In Lindstedt's view, who is to blame for the Oklahoma City bombing?

Reprinted from Martin Lindstedt, "UnCommon Sense," *Southwest Missouri Libertarian*, July/August 1995, by permission of the author.

Between the Revolutionary War's opening shots fired at Concord & Lexington on April 19, 1775 and the Declaration of Independence on July 4, 1776, the Founding Fathers and the citizenry had to make a decision as to whether they would negotiate with King George to restore their rights as Englishmen or seek to found a new nation. A man called Thomas Paine published on January 10, 1776 a small pamphlet called Common Sense. Colonists up and down the seaboard read his stirring call to action. George Washington himself said it turned doubt into decision—for independence.

This viewpoint's goal is to also turn doubt into decision—to restore a Constitutional Republic—by all and any means necessary.

REVOLUTION IS A RIGHT

This month [July 1995] we celebrated a holiday commemorating the Revolution which founded this country. The true meaning of the Declaration of Independence is Mankind's Right to Revolution. For example, examine these first key phrases of that document:

> When in the Course of human events, it becomes necessary for one people to dissolve the political bands which have connected them with another, and to assume among the powers of the earth, the separate and equal station to which the Laws of Nature and of Nature's God entitle them, a decent respect to the opinions of mankind requires that they should declare the causes which impel them to the separation.—We hold these truths to be self-evident, that all men are created equal, that they are endowed by their Creator with certain unalienable Rights, that among these are Life, Liberty and the pursuit of Happiness.— That to secure these rights, Governments are instituted among Men, deriving their just powers from the consent of the governed,—That whenever any Form of Government becomes destructive of these ends, it is the Right of the People to alter or to abolish it, and to institute new Government, laying its foundation on such principles and organizing its powers in such form, as to them shall seem most likely to effect their Safety and Happiness. Prudence, indeed, will dictate that Governments long established should not be changed for light and transient causes; and accordingly all experience hath shewn, that mankind are more disposed to suffer, while evils are sufferable, than to right themselves by abolishing the forms to which they are accustomed. But when a long train of abuses and usurpations, pursuing invariably the same Object evinces a design to reduce them under absolute Despotism, it is their right, it is their duty, to throw off such Government, and to provide new Guards for their future security.

I cannot sum up any better this relationship of the state as servant and the Individual as Master. If a person withdraws his consent from government, then government has no further right to control his actions, not that it ever did have a right to rule, only an obligation to serve and protect. That person can be said to have a Right to Revolution.

THE GOVERNMENT VIOLATES LAWS

The other great document which arose from the First American Revolutionary War, the Constitution, is silent on what happens if one party, the one supposed to be weaker, starts violating the provisions of this social contract. It's no secret the government violates the Constitution and steals the lives, liberties, and property of its citizens. It's no longer bound by Law. The state will not respect the Individual unless the Individual has the power to destroy the state. Then it's too late. There's a simple reason why the Constitution is silent regarding government violation of Law: It's self-evident the older document, the Declaration of Independence, takes precedence. Then a person's Right to Revolution can no longer be delayed or denied.

The current system is based upon theft, not law. Social Security steals from the earnings of the young to give the elderly a pittance of what could have been retained savings. The educational system steals children from their parents and money from property owners to indoctrinate children to worship government. The poison fruits from this poison tree are illiteracy and barbarism. Politicians, bureaucrats, and judges produce new decrees enabling "government-enforcement" agencies to terrorize citizens with impunity, putting the lie to badges saying they "Protect and Serve." Huge national debts intended to enslave future generations—if they allow it—are run up by politicians to buy votes today. But the death of the current system is in sight. Soon there will be nothing left to steal, as bands of degenerate looters roam the land, clawing for dwindling means of survival, and honest men produce only what they can defend.

Although the present regime pretends to be a democracy where the people rule, what happens when people withdraw their consent, their persons and property from government clutches? We know full well the consequences of taking back our freedoms. Our property is seized by the Internal Revenue Service (IRS). We might spend some time in jail. We might even be murdered by government agents. Ask Randy Weaver or the ghosts of one of the Koresh children.

Today, if you would be free, you better figure out the costs involved. Once you choose freedom, your only choices will be either to knuckle under for the moment or fight. But once you start knuckling under, then you will do it again, because cowardice is habit-forming and you probably won't fight until you are cornered like a rat. He who lives by running away, lives to run another day. If you choose to fight, then you will have to keep fighting until either the enemy is dead or you are. There is no resigning from the underground.

Every day when I hear government officials lying about their crimes, from the First Crook on down to the local policeman, I detect the tone of "You must believe this because you must." I am supposed to become an accomplice in their thefts, kidnappings and murders by the act of willfully believing outright lies. Supposedly, patriotism consists of condoning government crime because the government does all this for me and in my name. Well, I'm not buying this evil nonsense any more. Government is a fictional entity created in our own minds, and since we create it willingly in our own minds, we find it beautiful. But the reality is a nightmare, and the actors are evil men doing evil for its own sake, believing themselves safe from any accountability. No more! No more!

The government is morally, mentally, and financially bankrupt. It forces free men to hand over further credit at gunpoint. Civilization is breaking down. The future is one vast grey cloud of totalitarianism from here to the horizon. These now and future great hurts seem bearable only to those who would benefit from them. For the rest of us, enough is enough, and we will not suffer any more wrongs, simply because things were better in the past. Now we will fight, and bring about a different, hopefully better future.

GOVERNMENT HAS WORSENED

For every single evil against which the founding fathers rebelled, we have allowed ten.

Taxes? Even King George III didn't dare impose an income tax. The colonists threw subsidized, cheaper, better tea than the smuggled stuff into Boston Harbor. The colonists rebelled over total taxes of less than five percent per person. Compare that to the 70 percent taxation of today.

Loss of Liberty? This country imprisons over 1.3 million people and we have just beaten Russia as the country which imprisons the most of its citizens per capita. Over one half of one percent of our citizens are in jails. Some of them deserve to be in prison. But most of them are in prison not because they violated another human being's life, liberty, or property but because they didn't obey the government monster's latest whim.

Government murder? George III's redcoats only killed five Bostonians at the Boston Massacre, and they had to undergo trial. How many people were killed at the Waco Holocaust by the "government-enforcers" of our day using flame-throwing tanks? Ninety-some men, women, and children. The rascals responsible have not only not been tried for murder, they got promoted. The rest of us get to see unhung murderers investigating themselves and smarmily telling us that "Mistakes were made, but they brought it upon themselves." Ignored is the fact gun-control laws violate the Constitution and are nothing more than a power grab by cowardly Fascists who dislike the idea of being shot or hung by an enraged populace. These cowardly jack-booted government thugs went ballistic because the trapped Da-

---

THE GOVERNMENT HAS DESTROYED AMERICA

It's not just the Waco massacre or the bombing of Baghdad or this country's criminal policy in the Middle East which makes so many Americans hate their government. It's what the government has done to America.

It's the government's deliberate flooding of our country with non-Whites from the Third World, and the refusal to halt the massive illegal immigration across our border with Mexico and the Caribbean.

It's the government's catering to the worst elements in the population, buying their votes with welfare programs paid for by our hard work.

It's the government's theft of our freedom—with ever more oppressive taxes, with ever more restrictive rules and regulations of one sort or another, with efforts to take away our right to protect ourselves and our families.

It's the more and more obviously corrupt and degenerate politicians who are holding the highest offices in the government: crooks and liars of the sort typified by Bill Clinton. . . .

To yuppies in New York and Washington, none of these things may seem very important. For people who have never had an unfashionable thought in their heads, for people who turn to their television for all of their opinions and attitudes, it may be hard to understand why anyone would be upset about what the government has done to America. But, believe me, there are plenty of people who are very upset.

William L. Pierce, *Free Speech*, May 1995.

---

vidians shot back. They lied about drug labs in order to use tanks, and soon after the fire destroyed the evidence. They cut those people off from outside contact, and now that they are dead, they can make up whatever story they please about the people they killed. Government agencies investigated themselves and we are supposed to believe the resulting whitewash? The Nazis, the Communists and George III, for all their faults, were far more honest.

Now Oklahoma City comes up and we are supposed to believe government's continually changing stories and how targeted Patriot groups are responsible for the bombing. When you look at factors of ability, opportunity, and who benefits from this crime, there can be only one credible suspect: Criminal Government. By trying to blame the armed citizenry for this crime, we see not the beginning, but the middle of the beginning of a great civil war between the people and their would-be kings.

THE PERSPECTIVE OF THOMAS PAINE

What would Thomas Paine have to say, if he were alive today, about the actions of the degenerate government of our time? Perhaps we can look at what he had to say about King George III after his troops burned down Portland, Maine in the winter of 1775 and drove the inhabitants out to freeze.

> Men of passive tempers look somewhat lightly over the offenses of Britain, {government} and, still hoping for the best, are apt to call out, Come we shall be friends again for all this. But examine the passions and feelings of mankind. Bring the doctrine of reconciliation to the touchstone of nature, and then tell me, whether you can hereafter love, honor, and faithfully serve the power that hath carried fire and sword into your land? If you cannot do all these, then are you only deceiving yourselves, and by your delay bringing ruin upon posterity. Your future connection with Britain, {government} whom you can neither love nor honor, will be forced and unnatural, and being formed only on the plan of present convenience, will in a little time fall into a relapse more wretched than the first. But if you say, you can still pass the violations {by government} over, then I ask, Hath your house been burnt? Hath your property been destroyed before your face? Are your wife and children destitute of a bed to lie on, or bread to live on? Have you lost a parent or a child by their hands, and yourself the ruined and wretched survivor? If you have not, then are you not a judge of those who have. But if you have, and can still shake hands with the murderers, then are you unworthy the name of husband, father, friend, or lover, and whatever may be your rank or title in life, you have the heart of a coward, and the spirit of a sycophant.

Reconciliation is a fallacious dream. Nature hath deserted the connection, and Art cannot supply her place. For, as Milton wisely expresses, "never can true reconcilement grow where wounds of deadly hate have pierced so deep."

No man was a warmer wisher for reconciliation than myself, before the fatal nineteenth of April, 1775 (Massacre at Lexington), {Ruby Ridge, Waco, and Oklahoma City, April 19, 1992, 1993, 1995} but the moment the event of that day was made known, I rejected the hardened, sullen tempered Pharaoh of England {Washington} for ever; and disdain the wretch, that with the pretended title of Father of his people, can unfeelingly hear of their slaughter, and composedly sleep with their blood upon his soul. . .

I have heard some men say, many of whom I believe spoke without thinking, that they dreaded independence {freedom}, fearing that it would produce civil wars. It is but seldom that our first thoughts are truly correct, and that is the case here; for there are ten times more to dread from a patched up connection than from independence. I make the sufferers' case my own, and I protest, that were I driven from house and home, my property destroyed, and my circumstances ruined, that as man, sensible of injuries, I could never relish the doctrine of reconciliation, or consider myself bound thereby. . . .

Every day wears out the little remains of kindred between us and them, and can there be any reason to hope, that as the relationship expires, the affection will increase, or that we shall agree better, when we have ten times more and greater concerns to quarrel over than ever?

Ye that tell us of harmony and reconciliation, can ye restore to us the time that is past? Can ye give to prostitution its former innocence? Neither can ye reconcile Britain {the government} and America {the people}. . .

We fight neither for revenge nor conquest; neither from pride nor passion; we are not insulting the world with our fleets and armies, nor ravaging the globe for plunder. Beneath the shade of our own vines are we attacked; in our own houses, and on our own lands, is the violence committed against us. We view our enemies {terrorcrat government enforcers} in the characters of highwaymen and housebreakers {houseburners}, and having no defence for ourselves in the civil law; are obliged to punish them by the military one, and apply the sword {rifle}, in the very case, where you have before now, applied the halter {rope}.

This Paine was no Uncle Tom. He saw what needed to be done, so he urged his countrymen to exercise their Right and fulfill their Duty, and so they waged their Revolution.

"I say this to the militias . . . If you
say violence is an acceptable way to
make change, you are wrong."

VIOLENCE AGAINST THE
GOVERNMENT IS NOT JUSTIFIED

Bill Clinton

The following viewpoint is excerpted from remarks made by Bill
Clinton at the May 5, 1995, commencement ceremony at Michigan State University. In his speech, Clinton asserts that violence
against the government, such as the bombing in Oklahoma City,
is not justified. Militia members and others who view government and its employees as a threat to their freedom are mis-
guided, he asserts. He contends that while Americans have the
right to disagree with the government and to work within the
law to change government policies, violent protest is not acceptable. Clinton is the 42nd president of the United States.

As you read, consider the following questions:

1. What is the security challenge of the 21st century, according
   to Clinton?
2. In the president's view, how does the Constitution limit the
   abuse of government power?
3. According to Clinton, who are the real American heroes?

Excerpted from Bill Clinton's commencement speech at Michigan State University, East
Lansing, Michigan, May 5, 1995.

You who are graduating will have the chance to live in the most exciting, the most prosperous, the most diverse and interesting world in the entire history of humanity. Still you must face the fact that no time is free of problems, and we have new and grave security challenges.

SOCIETY FACES MANY CHALLENGES

In this, the 20th century, millions of lives were lost in wars between nations, and in efforts by totalitarian dictatorships to stamp out the light of liberty among their subjects. In the 21st century, bloody wars of ethnic and tribal hatred will be fought still in some parts of the world. But with freedom and democracy advancing, the real threat to our security will be rooted in the fact that all the forces that are lifting us up and opening unparalleled opportunity for us contain a dark underside. For open societies are characterized by free and rapid movements of people and technology and information. And that very wonder makes them very, very vulnerable to the forces of organized destruction and evil. So the great security challenge for your future in the 21st century will be to determine how to beat back the dangers while keeping the benefits of this new time.

The dark possibilities of our age are visible now in the smoke, the horror and the heartbreak of Oklahoma City. As the long and painful search and rescue effort comes to an end with 165 dead, 467 injured, and two still unaccounted for, our prayers are with those who lost their loved ones, and with the brave and good people of Oklahoma City, who have moved with such strength and character to deal with this tragedy.

But that threat is not isolated. And you must not believe it is. We see that threat again in the bombing of the World Trade Center in New York; in the nerve gas attack in the Tokyo subway; in the terrorist assault on innocent civilians in the Middle East; in the organized crime plaguing the former Soviet Union now that the heavy hand of communism has been lifted. We see it even on the Internet, where people exchange information about bombs and terrorism, even as children learn from sources all around the world.

PRESERVING SAFETY AND FREEDOM

My fellow Americans, we must respond to this threat in ways that preserve both our security and our freedoms. Appeasement of organized evil is not an option for the 21st century any more than it was in this century. Like the vigilant generations that brought us victory in World War II and the Cold War, we must stand our ground. In this high-tech world, we must make sure that we have the high-tech tools to confront the high-tech forces of destruction and evil. . . .

We can do this without undermining our constitutional rights. In fact, the failure to act will undermine those rights. For no one is free in America where parents have to worry when they drop off their children for day care, or when you are the target of assassination simply because you work for our government. No one is free in America when large numbers of our fellow citizens must always be looking over their shoulders.

MISGUIDED MILITIA BELIEFS

It is with this in mind that I would like to say something to the paramilitary groups and to others who believe the greatest threat to America comes not from terrorists from within our country or beyond our borders, but from our own government.

I want to say this to the militias and to others who believe this, to those nearby and those far away: I am well aware that most of you have never violated the law of the land. I welcome the comments that some of you have made condemning the bombing in Oklahoma City. I believe you have every right, indeed you have the responsibility, to question our government when you disagree with its policies. And I will do everything in my power to protect your right to do so.

But I also know there have been lawbreakers among those who espouse your philosophy. I know from painful personal experience as a governor of a state who lived through the cold-blooded killing of a young sheriff and a young African American state trooper who were friends of mine by people who espouse the view that the government was the biggest problem in America and that people had a right to take violence into their own hands.

So I ask you to hear me now. It is one thing to believe that the federal government has too much power and to work within the law to reduce it. It is quite another to break the law of the land and threaten to shoot officers of the law if all they do is their duty to uphold it.

It is one thing to believe we are taxed too much and work to reduce the tax burden. It is quite another to refuse to pay your taxes, though your neighbor pays his. It is one thing to believe we are over-regulated and to work to lessen the burden of regulation. It is quite another to slander our dedicated public servants, our brave police officers, even our rescue workers who have been called a hostile army of occupation.

This is a very free country. Those of you in the militia movements have broader rights here than you would in any other country in the entire world.

Violence Is Not a Right

Do people who work for the government sometimes make mistakes? Of course they do. They are human. Almost every American has some experience with this—a rude tax collector, an arbitrary regulator, an insensitive social worker, an abusive law officer. As long as human beings make up our government there will be mistakes. But our Constitution was established by Americans determined to limit those abuses. And think of the limits—the Bill of Rights, the separation of powers, access to the courts, the right to take your case to the country through the media, and the right to vote people in or out of office on a regular basis.

But there is no right to resort to violence when you don't get your way. There is no right to kill people. There is no right to kill people who are doing their duty, or minding their own business, or children who are innocent in every way. Those are the people who perished in Oklahoma City. And those who claim such rights are wrong and un-American.

Whenever in our history people have believed that violence is a legitimate extension of politics they have been wrong. In the 1960s, . . . many good things happened and there was much turmoil. But the Weathermen of the radical left who resorted to violence in the 1960s were wrong. Today, the gang members who use life on the mean streets of America, as terrible as it is, to justify taking the law into their own hands and taking innocent life are wrong. The people who came to the United States to bomb the World Trade Center were wrong.

Freedom of political speech will never justify violence— never. Our founding fathers created a system of laws in which reason could prevail over fear. Without respect for this law there is no freedom.

So I say this to the militias and all others who believe that the greatest threat to freedom comes from the government instead of from those who would take away our freedom: If you say violence is an acceptable way to make change, you are wrong. If you say that government is in a conspiracy to take your freedom away, you are just plain wrong.

Hating America Is Not Patriotic

If you treat law enforcement officers who put their lives on the line for your safety every day like some kind of enemy army to be suspected, derided and, if they should enforce the law against you, to be shot, you are wrong. If you appropriate our sacred symbols for paranoid purposes and compare yourselves to colonial militias who fought for the democracy you now rail against, you are wrong.

How dare you suggest that we in the freest nation on Earth live in tyranny. How dare you call yourselves patriots and heroes.

America Is Not a Tyranny

Our nation's Founders were not anti-intellectual opponents of government as such. Through our Constitution, they in fact *established* one with the positive aim of preserving and protecting individual rights. That's because they understood the vital connection between *individual rights* and *the rule of law*. Undermine the latter, and you jeopardize the former.

We in America do not live under pure laissez-faire; far from it. But we also do not live under tyranny. To contend otherwise trivializes the full horror of real tyranny. Here, we can write, speak, and vote freely. Regulated we are, but not enslaved.

Robert James Bidinotto, *Freeman*, July 1995.

I say to you, all of you, the members of the Class of 1995, there is nothing patriotic about hating your country, or pretending that you can love your country but despise your government. There is nothing heroic about turning your back on America, or ignoring your own responsibilities. If you want to preserve your own freedom, you must stand up for the freedom of others with whom you disagree. But you also must stand up for the rule of law. You cannot have one without the other.

The real American heroes today are the citizens who get up every morning and have the courage to work hard and play by the rules—the mother who stays up the extra half hour after a long day's work to read her child a story; the rescue worker who digs with his hands in the rubble as the building crumbles about him; the neighbor who lives side-by-side with people different from himself; the government worker who quietly and efficiently labors to see to it that the programs we depend on are honestly and properly carried out; most of all, the parent who works long years for modest pay and sacrifices so that his or her children can have the education that you have had, and the chances you are going to have. I ask you never to forget that.

And I would like to say one word to the people of the United States. I know you have heard a lot of publicity in recent days about Michigan and militias. But what you have seen and heard is not the real Michigan. This is the real Michigan. . . .

A Promising Future

So, my fellow Americans and members of the Class of 1995, let me close by reminding you once again that you live in a very great country. When we are united by our humanity and our civic virtue, nothing can stop us. Let me remind you once again that our best days as a nation still lie before us. But we must not give in to fear or use the frustrations of the moment as an excuse to walk from the obligations of citizenship.

Remember what our founding fathers built. Remember the victories won for us in the Cold War and in World War II, 50 years ago next week. Remember the blood and sweat and triumph that enabled us to come to this, the greatest moment of possibility in our history.

Go out and make the most of the potential God has given you. Make the most of the opportunities and freedoms America has given to you. Be optimistic; be strong. Make the choices that Theodore Roosevelt made, that Ernest Green made. Seize your moment. Build a better future. And redeem once again the promise of America.

| "When Irish people have taken up the armed struggle, they had right on their side."

RESISTANCE TO BRITISH RULE JUSTIFIES BOMBINGS IN NORTHERN IRELAND

Mark O'Connell

In the following viewpoint, Mark O'Connell presents the view of Martin Galvin, who argues that bombings in Northern Ireland, such as the August 15, 1998, incident in Omagh, can be justified in the name of protesting British rule in the northern counties. Galvin, the former publicity director for the American-based Irish Northern Aid Committee, contends that physical force by the Real Irish Republican Army (RIRA)—a dissident group made up of former members of the Irish Republican Army but not affiliated with the IRA—in response to actions by Britain's government is morally legitimate. O'Connell is the political correspondent for the *Sunday Business Post*, an Irish newspaper.

As you read, consider the following questions:

1. What does Galvin claim is the goal of the Good Friday Agreement, as cited by O'Connell?
2. According to Galvin, what are some of the pledges that have been broken by the British government?
3. Why is Galvin concerned about the increased powers given to the Royal Ulster Constabulary?

Reprinted from Mark O'Connell, "Noraid's Galvin Has Doubts on RIRA," *The Sunday Business Post*, September 13, 1998, by permission of the author.

M artin Galvin, the Irish-American lawyer and former Irish Northern Aid Committee (Noraid) publicity director, believes the Real Irish Republican Army (RIRA) ceasefire might not be permanent. He also says that Britain's "capacity to provoke injustice" might yet provide the moral basis on which to resume the "armed struggle."

MARTIN GALVIN'S VIEWS

Galvin, who refused to condemn the Omagh bombing in which 29 people were killed in August 1998 described himself as a supporter of the 32 County Sovereignty Committee, an organisation associated in the media with the Real IRA. [The committee is an Irish Republican group opposed to the peace process.]

He claimed the Good Friday Agreement [a peace agreement reached in April 1998] was a trap to co-opt republicans into a system which consolidated British rule in Ireland.

"Either the Stormont deal will be the undoing of an unjust system or it will contribute to the reinforcement of British rule in Ireland," he said. [Stormont was the location in Belfast, Northern Ireland, where the peace agreement was reached.]

"People will soon see that David Trimble [the head of the Ulster Unionist party] was right when he said that the agreement would make the union safer. If the unionists wanted to facilitate a more just society, you would not see the sort of sectarian dynamic which is central to the agreement.

"The deal states that if the unionists lose their majority, the six counties will become part of a united Ireland.

"But I do not believe the unionists and the British government would follow through on this when the nationalist parties are in the majority. All the pledges they have made about fair employment, a proper system of justice and police reform have been broken. There is no reason to believe they are going to change."

PHYSICAL FORCE AND MORAL JUSTIFICATION

While he did not want to be quoted as a spokesman on behalf of the RIRA, he said the organisation's statement was noteworthy for the omission of the word permanent.

"I have never encouraged people to use violence, but when Irish people have taken up the armed struggle, they had right on their side.

"Physical force can only be used in accordance with a moral code.

"In the years from 1969 till the ceasefires, the Provisional IRA was morally justified in its armed struggle. Using the same logic, I see no reason why the use of violence could not be justified in the future.

"British rule has provoked a morally unjustifiable system which has generated conflict for years. Anybody who says that British rule does not have the capacity to provoke further armed tension in the future is being naive and unrealistic. I am not privy to the thinking in the Real IRA, but I haven't seen anything in its statement to suggest that the cessation is permanent, or not."

GALVIN'S CRITICISMS

Galvin, whose forebears come from Offaly, lives and practises as an attorney in New York. He strongly criticised the threats made by republicans against members of the 32 County Sovereignty Committee.

"The 32 County Sovereignty Committee is a legitimate political entity.

ARMED STRUGGLE IS LEGITIMATE

1. During the Home Rule crisis of 1912 it was the British and loyalist forces which threatened and used violence against the reunification of Ireland. This was followed by 50 years of state oppression of the nationalist community including attacks and pogroms by state forces. In this present phase of armed struggle, state violence and armed conflict predated the IRA campaign.

2. The Civil Rights campaign of the 1960s was brutally attacked by the forces of the state, official and unofficial.

3. The British army was sent in not to protect the nationalists but to shore up unionism in the rest of Britain.

4. From 1969–'71 the nationalist community was subjected to repeated RUC/loyalists/British army attacks.

5. 90% of deaths caused by loyalists have been civilians. 55% of those killed by the British army have been civilians.

6. Armed struggle throughout history has been seen as a legitimate part of a people's resistance to foreign oppression.

7. Armed struggle for republicans is an option of last resort.

8. There is no constitutional strategy to pursue national independence.

9. The onus is on those who condemn armed struggle to advance a credible alternative.

Irish Northern Aid Committee, "Towards a Lasting Peace in Ireland: Overview." Available at http://inac.org/history/guide.html.

"It is sad to see threats being made against its members by Sinn Fein members. [Sinn Fein is an Irish Republican political party.]

"Violence between republican groups can only serve British interests.

"We have heard the announcement that [Sinn Fein chief negotiator] Martin McGuinness is to take part in the decommissioning body, we have seen the threats made to members of the 32 County Sovereignty Committee and we have noted the words formulated by [the president of Sinn Fein] Gerry Adams, who said that in effect the war was over. This is not good.

"I hope I am wrong, but all I see tells me that republicans are being co-opted into securing British rule in Ireland."

DANGEROUS POWERS

He was deeply concerned that the Royal Ulster Constabulary (RUC) had been given unprecedented powers by the British government and he criticised the emergency legislation enacted following the Omagh bombings by the Oireachtas [Ireland's parliament]. [The RUC is the police force of Northern Ireland.]

"Instead of reforming the RUC by disbanding it, the British government is giving it more powers, powers which allow the word of an RUC officer not just to arrest but to convict a suspect.

"These powers will be used against political dissidents and other innocent people."

"[The Real Irish Republican Army
(RIRA)] must disband and call off
their unforgiveable and unjustifiable
campaign of action."

BOMBINGS IN NORTHERN IRELAND CANNOT BE JUSTIFIED

Andersonstown News

In the following viewpoint, the *Andersonstown News* contends that the August 15, 1998, bombing in Omagh, Northern Ireland, that killed twenty-nine people was not justified. The newspaper asserts that the attack served no political purpose since peace has almost been achieved in Northern Ireland. In addition, the newspaper argues, the group responsible for the bombing—the Real Irish Republican Army (RIRA, an organization consisting of former members of the Provisional IRA but unaffiliated with the latter group)—lacks support within Northern Ireland and should end its activities. The *Andersonstown News* is a weekly newspaper published in Belfast, Northern Ireland.

As you read, consider the following questions:

1. According to the *Andersonstown News*, what motive is behind every action of the dissident republican groups?
2. How did support for the Provisional IRA vary in Belfast, according to the newspaper?
3. In the view of the *Andersonstown News*, why are the members of the RIRA and its supporters not true republicans?

Reprinted from "Stand Down Now, for All Our Sakes," editorial, *Andersonstown News*, August 22, 1998, by permission.

The death of 29 men, women and children in the Omagh bomb [an August 15, 1998, attack in Northern Ireland] is a human catastrophe of such proportions that it almost defies description. But when one factors in the climate in which it took place—republican and loyalist ceasefires in place and the prospect of real peace so tantalisingly within our grasp—the pain becomes almost unbearable.

THE REAL IRA MUST DISBAND

Now that the prayers have been said and the candles lit, the time for reflection and analysis has arrived. Millions of words have already been said and written, millions more are to come. But when it comes right down to it, the essence of the matter can be distilled into a brief sentence directed towards the Real Irish Republican Army (RIRA): Stop what you're doing and stop it now.

The Real IRA has declared a suspension of operations and has offered a craven apology for what it did in Omagh. This is not good enough. They must disband and call off their unforgiveable and unjustifiable campaign of action. . . . In a community which has suffered more than most from the iron fist of heavy security, it seems almost impossible that there would be any support for the kind of security measures currently being suggested to combat the Real IRA. But support there is, and strong support too. Those responsible for the Omagh bomb, and those [who] would give them support, should reflect on what that says about them and about their organisation. [The Real IRA called a ceasefire in September 1998.]

It's not entirely clear, given the unbendable dogma which drives the dissident republican groups, whether the enormity of what happened in Omagh will have been enough to convince them of the folly of their ways. On a theoretical level—a dangerous level on which the Real IRA and the Continuity IRA operate—an atrocity on this scale makes no difference whatsoever to the drive-the-Brits-into-the-sea motive which drives every action of the dissident groups. Whether it has the power to move them as human beings is another question and one which will have its answer in the days and weeks to come.

SUPPORT FOR VIOLENCE HAS ENDED

Those whom the Real IRA and their political allies would hope to take with them as they embark on the road to nowhere are left sickened and appalled by what they have seen. If the prospects of that embryonic group winning enough support to allow it to expand its campaign were slim before Omagh, they

The Real IRA get to recognise the enemy

Heath. Reprinted by permission of *The Spectator*, London.

---

are nonexistent now. That may be cold comfort indeed, but it is something.

For 30 years this community provided a space within [which] the Provisional IRA grew and thrived. Not everyone supported the IRA, but many did. At one end of the scale, people provided active support in the form of safe houses and the like; at the other end, they turned a blind eye and pulled their curtains. They did so not because they had an innate disposition towards violence—far from it. Ordinary people found themselves caught up in an extraordinary situation and were forced to make choices. Morally and practically, there was a price to be paid. As lives were lost and blood flowed, people continually questioned what was going on around them but generally found a political and moral justification that allowed them to live with their choice.

In the homes of West Belfast, on the streets and in the pubs and clubs, you would be hard pushed to come across anyone able to find a shred of political or moral justification for what the Real IRA are doing. Anyone who could find it in his or her heart to offer support to the Real IRA is not likely to advertise the fact, this week or any other.

NOT TRUE REPUBLICANISM

Among nationalists and republicans, those who carried out this bombing and those who seek to justify it or refuse to condemn it, are reviled and rejected. Support for them is negligible and with this record behind them, they are not likely to change that. However much they claim the mantle of true republicanism, the fact is that their actions are being carried out on their own behalf and on behalf of no-one else.

So let's have none of this 'suspension' of violence wherein the Real IRA proposes to stand balefully in the shadows while the rest of us wonder whether they might not decide to do another Omagh when they feel the time is right.

The Real IRA should disband immediately and they should say so very loudly and very clearly. Then the rest of us can get on with the business of coming to terms with what that organisation did in its short and bloody history.

| "We believe that the biggest thieves in the world and the terrorists are the Americans."

AMERICAN POLICIES IN THE MIDDLE EAST JUSTIFY ISLAMIC TERRORISM

Osama Bin Ladin, interviewed by John Miller

The following viewpoint is excerpted from an interview with Saudi Arabian multimillionaire and alleged terrorist mastermind Osama Bin Ladin, conducted by ABC News correspondent John Miller. Bin Ladin argues that attacks by Muslims on Americans in Africa and the Middle East are justifiable responses to American terrorism. He contends that the policies of the U.S. government have led to the deaths of Arab civilians and must be answered in a similar fashion. Bin Ladin asserts that the goal of Islam is to win a jihad that will lead to the removal of all Americans from Muslim land.

As you read, consider the following questions:

1. How many Iraqi children died due to American sanctions, according to testimony cited by Bin Ladin?
2. According to Bin Ladin, who are Muslims forbidden to kill?
3. What is Bin Ladin's message to the American people?

Excerpted from "Talking with Terror's Banker," an interview of Osama Bin Ladin by John Miller, ABC News transcript, www.abcnews.com. Reprinted by permission of ABC News, New York.

John Miller: Mr. Bin Ladin, to Americans you are an interesting figure: A man who comes from a background of wealth and comforts who ended up fighting on the front lines. Many Americans would think that's unusual.

Osama Bin Ladin: Thanks be to Allah. It is hard for one to understand if the person does not understand Islam. In our religion we believe that Allah created us to worship him. Allah is the one who created us and blessed us with this religion, and orders us to carry out the holy struggle "jihad" to raise the word of Allah above the words of the unbelievers.

We believe this is a form of worship we must follow despite our financial ability. This is a response to Westerners and secularists in the Arab world who claim the reason for the awakening and the return to Islam is financial difficulties. This is untrue. In fact, the return of the people to Islam is a blessing from Allah, and their return is a need for Allah.

This is not a strange issue. During the days of jihad, thousands of young men who were well off financially left the Arabian Peninsula and other areas and joined the fighting—hundreds of them were killed in Afghanistan, Bosnia and Chechnya. We pray Allah grants them martyr status.

American Opinion Is Irrelevant

You have been described as the "World's Most Wanted Man." There is word that the American government intends to put a price on your head in the millions for your capture. Do you think about that? Does it worry you?

Praise be to Allah. It does not worry us what the Americans think. What worries us is pleasing Allah. The Americans impose themselves on everyone who believes in his religion and his rights. They accuse our children in Palestine of being terrorists. Those children that have no weapons and have not even reached maturity. At the same time they defend a country with its airplanes and tanks, and the state of the Jews, that has a policy to destroy the future of these children.

Bill Clinton stands after Qana and defends the horrible massacre that severed the heads of children and killed about 100 persons. Clinton stands and claims Israel has the right to defend itself. We do not worry about American opinion, or the fact they place prices on our heads. [In April 1996, Israel bombed a United Nations refugee camp in Qana, Lebanon. Israel claimed the bombs were intended for a different target.]

We as Muslims believe that our fate is set. If the whole world decides to get together and kill us before our time has come, we will not die, our livelihood is set. No matter how much pressure America places on the regime in Riyadh [the royal capital of

Saudi Arabia] to freeze our assets and to prevent people from contributing to this great cause, we rely on Allah.

You have said, "If the Americans are so brave they will come and arrest me." Do you think that is something my country will try?

We have seen in the last decade the decline of the American government and the weakness of the American soldier who is ready to wage Cold Wars and unprepared to fight long wars. This was proven in Beirut when the Marines fled after two explosions. It also proves they can run in less than 24 hours, and this was also repeated in Somalia. We are ready for all occasions. We rely on Allah.

AMERICANS SHOULD BE PUNISHED

Mr. Bin Ladin, you have issued a fatwa [religious ruling] calling on all Muslims to kill Americans where they can, when they can. Is that directed at all Americans, just American military, just Americans in Saudi Arabia?

As we mentioned before, Allah ordered us in this religion to purify Muslim land of all non-believers, and especially the Arabian Peninsula where the Ke'ba is. After WWII, the Americans became more aggressive and oppressive, especially in the Muslim world.

We are surprised this question is coming from Americans. Each action will solicit a similar reaction. We must use such punishment to keep your evil away from Muslims, Muslim children and women. American history does not distinguish between civilians and military, and not even women and children. They are the ones who used the bombs against Nagasaki. Can these bombs distinguish between infants and military? America does not have a religion that will prevent it from destroying all people.

Your situation with Muslims in Palestine is shameful, if there is any shame left in America. In the Sabra and Shatilla massacre, a cooperation between Zionist and Christian forces, houses were demolished over the heads of children. Also, by testimony of relief workers in Iraq, the American-led sanctions resulted in the death of over 1 million Iraqi children. [Sabra and Shatilla were camps south of Beirut, Lebanon, and the site of a 1982 massacre of Palestinians.]

All of this was done in the name of American interests. We believe that the biggest thieves in the world and the terrorists are the Americans. The only way for us to fend off these assaults is to use similar means.

We do not differentiate between those dressed in military uniforms and civilians; they are all targets in this fatwa. Especially since American officials were released after the Khobar bombing, asking all American civilians to contact the security department in the embassy with information on Muslims and activists. The fatwa includes all that share or take part in killing of Muslims, assaulting holy places, or those who help the Jews occupy Muslim land. . . .

FIGHTING FOR ALLAH

You have been painted in America as a terrorist leader. To your followers you are a hero. How do you see yourself?

As I said before, we do not worry about what America says. We look at ourselves and our brethren as worshipers of Allah who created us to worship him and follow his books and prophets. I am one of Allah's worshipers. I worship Allah, which includes carrying out the jihad to raise Allah's word and evict the Americans from all Muslim land.

No one expected the mujahideen to defeat the Russians in Afghanistan. That caused a surprise to everyone. What do you see as the future for the American involvement in the Middle East and taking on groups like yours?

The North Atlantic Treaty Organization (NATO), that America created, we know it spent $455 billion American dollars in improving weaponry to protect Europe and America from Russia, and they did not fire a single shot. Allah stood with the Muslims, the Afghani mujahideen, and those who fought with them from other Muslim countries. We fought against the Russians and the Soviet Union until, not to say we defeated them, but Allah defeated them, they became nonexistent. There is a lesson to learn from this for he who wishes to learn.

The Soviet Union entered in the last week of 1979, in December, and with Allah's help their flag was folded December 25 a few years later and thrown in the trash, and there was nothing left to call Soviet Union.

We are sure of Allah's victory and our victory against the Americans and the Jews as promised by the prophet peace be up on him: "Judgment day shall not come until the Muslims fight the Jews, whereas the Jews will hide behind trees and stones, and the tree and the stone will speak and say 'Muslim, behind me a Jew come and kill him,' except for the al-Ghargad tree, which is a Jewish plant."

We are sure of our victory. Our battle with the Americans is larger than our battle with the Russians. . . .

We predict a black day for America and the end of the United States as United States, and will be separate states, and will retreat from our land and collect the bodies of its sons back to America. Allah willing. . . .

Describe the situation when your men took on the Americans in Somalia. Were you there?

After Allah honored us with victory in Afghanistan, and justice prevailed and the killing of those who slaughtered millions of Muslims in the Muslim republics, it cleared from Muslim minds the myth of superpowers. The youth ceased from seeing America as a superpower. After leaving Afghanistan they headed for Somalia and prepared for a long battle, thinking that the Americans were like the Russians, but they were surprised when the Americans entered with 300,000 troops, and collected more troops from the world—5,000 from Pakistan, 5,000 from India, 5,000 from Bangladesh, 5,000 from Egypt, Senegal and others like Saudi Arabia.

The youth were surprised at the low morale of the American soldiers and realized more than before that the America soldiers are paper tigers. After a few blows, they ran in defeat and America forgot about all the hoopla and media propaganda after leaving the Gulf War and destroying infrastructure—and destroying baby formula factories, all civilian factories, bridges and dams that help planting food—about being the world leader, and the leader of the new world order. After a few blows, they forgot about this title and left, dragging their corpses and their shameful defeat and stopped using such titles. And they learned in America that this name is larger than them.

When this took place, I was in Sudan, and this great defeat pleased me very much, the way it pleases all Muslims.

Allah willing the next victory will be in Hejaz and Najd, Saudi Arabia, and it will make the Americans forget the horrors of Vietnam and Beirut.

UNDIFFERENTIATED SLAUGHTER

Many Americans believe that fighting army to army like what happened in Afghanistan is heroic for either army, but setting off bombs killing civilians and innocents like the World Trade Center is terrorism.

He is using talk that they are not following. After our victory in Afghanistan and defeating the Russians, the world media, led by the American media, started a campaign against us that is still going on today despite the fact that the Russians left in 1989. They have carried out this campaign accusing us of being terrorists without any action being taken by the mujahideen against the real terrorists, the Americans. That is one side.

On the other side, American policy does not admit to differentiating between civilians, military, and child, human or animal. Examples I mentioned before are Nagasaki and Hiroshima where they tried to eliminate a whole people.

When it comes to Muslims, there is testimony from Western-ers and Christians who testified to the death of hundreds of thousands of our children in Iraq. And there is Qana, Sabra and Shattila, Dir Yasin and Bosnia. [Dir Yasin was a 1948 massacre in which 200 Palestinians were killed.]

The crusaders continued their slaughter of our mothers, sis-ters and children. America every time makes a decision to sup-port them and prevent weapons from reaching the Muslims, and allow Serbian butchers to slaughter Muslims.

You do not have a religion that prevents you from carrying out these actions and therefore you do not have the right to ob-ject to like treatment. Every action solicits a reaction. It is a pun-ishment that fits the crime. At the same time, our primary targets are military and those in its employment.

Our religion forbids us to kill innocents—children, women who are not combatants. Women soldiers who place themselves in the battle trenches receive the same treatment as fighting men.

COORDINATING A JIHAD

Is there a high council of the leaders of different groups like yours that decides on ways and means to attack Americans?

After the Americans entered the Holy Land, many emotions were roused in the Muslim world, more than we have seen be-fore. A great meeting took place in May 1998 in Pakistan, and it was attended by 150 scholars in Pakistan. The goal of the meet-ing was to work toward liberating the Holy Land and coordinate efforts between Muslim masses in the area.

Also, with Allah's blessings, scholars from Afghanistan, India and other Muslim nations' individual fatwas were passed, but here great joint fatwas were passed. The cooperation is expand-ing between general supporters of this religion. From this effort, the International Islamic Front for the Jihad Against Jews and Crusaders was formed, which we are a member of with other groups. It has a higher council to coordinate rousing the Muslim nation to carry out jihad against the Jews and the crusaders.

The American people by the large do not know the name Osama Bin Ladin, but they soon will. Do you have a message to the American people?

I say that the American people gave leadership to a traitorous leadership. This became very clear and especially in Clinton's gov-ernment. The American government, we think, is an agent that represents the Israel inside America. If we look at sensitive de-partments in the present government like the defense department or the state department, or sensitive security departments like the

CIA and others, we find that Jews have the first word in the American government, which is how they use America to carry out their plans in the world and especially the Muslim world.

A FATWA AGAINST AMERICANS

The ruling to kill the Americans and their allies—civilians and military—is an individual duty for every Muslim who can do it in any country in which it is possible to do it, in order to liberate the al-Aqsa Mosque and the holy mosque [Mecca] from their grip, and in order for their armies to move out of all the lands of Islam, defeated and unable to threaten any Muslim. This is in accordance with the words of Almighty God, "and fight the pagans all together as they fight you all together," and "fight them until there is no more tumult or oppression, and there prevail justice and faith in God."

World Islamic Front, "Jihad Against Jews and Crusaders," February 23, 1998.

The presence of Americans in the Holy Land supports the Jews and gives them a safe back. The American government, in a time where there are millions of Americans living on the street and those living below the standard of living and below the poverty line, we find the American government turning toward helping Israel in occupying our land and building settlements in the Holy Land.

The American government is throwing away the lives of Americans in Saudi Arabia for the interests of the Jews. The Jews are a people who Allah cited in his holy book the Koran as those who attacked prophets with lies and killings, and attacked Mary and accused her of a great sin. They are a people who killed Allah's prophets—would they not kill, rape and steal from humans?

They believe that all humans are created for their use, and found that the Americans are the best-created beings for that use. The American Government is driving America to destruction and those same ones have no doubts about America being a superpower in the next decade.

So, we tell the Americans as a people, and we tell the mothers of soldiers, and American mothers in general, if they value their lives and those of their children, find a nationalistic government that will look after their interests and not the interest of the Jews.

The continuation of the tyranny will bring the fighting to America, like Ramzi Yousef and others. This is my message to the American people to look for a serious government that looks out for their interest and does not attack others, their lands or their honor.

AMERICA'S GOVERNMENT IS AT FAULT

Mr. Bin Ladin, these are most of the questions we came with. Is there anything else that I did not ask that you would like to add?

We would like to stress that we are on close contact with Muslim masses, praise be to Allah. The issue of liberating Holy Lands is not my personal desire, but I am just a worshiper of Allah and one of Allah's soldiers in the Muslim nation.

The movement is driving fast and light forward. And I am sure of our victory with Allah's help against America and the Jews. We see this then in the strength of the reaction, that every day the Americans delay their departure, for every day they delay, they will receive a new corpse from Muslim countries.

The Saudi Arabian government captured a few months ago in Ramadan a number of missiles, anti aircraft missiles, surface-to-air missile (SAM) and stinger missiles.

Can the America government explain to its people when a SAM missile is launched against a passenger military airplane with 250 soldiers aboard? Can they justify their deaths? What the Saudi Arabian government captured is much less than what was not captured. The American government, if it has anything left to hang on to, has no choice but to pull its sons from the Holy Land especially and the Muslim land in general. And to refrain from supporting in any way the Israeli government and Jews who occupy our land.

We place the complete responsibility on the American government of any attacks against Muslims and its support of regimes in our countries against the best interest of the people. We also hold them responsible for its attacks on Islamic symbols, Sheik Abdel Rahman, who is considered one of most prominent Islamic scholars who Allah gave the courage to speak the truth.

We hear that he is in a bad health condition, and he is a man beyond 60 years of age and is blind and America treats him badly. The imprisonment of Sheik Omar is an attack on the Muslim religion, and countries. We hold it completely responsible for the imprisonment of Sheik Omar and the imprisonment of other Muslims in America.

My word to American journalists is not to ask why we did that, but to ask what had their government done that forced us to defend ourselves?

This is all I have to say.

"Jihad with iron and fire is the only way to reclaim Palestine from the hands of the Jews."

ISRAELI OCCUPATION OF PALESTINE JUSTIFIES ISLAMIC TERRORISM

Nida'ul Islam

In the following viewpoint, Nida'ul Islam maintains that jihad, or a holy war, is justified in order to end Israel's occupation of Palestine. Nida'ul Islam contends that this violence is legitimate because Palestine is a Muslim country that should not be under the unlawful control of a Jewish nation. The magazine asserts that the Zionist [people who support the establishment of a Jewish homeland] government in Israel has sought domination of the Middle East and has used oppression, terrorism, and illegal peace treaties to destroy Palestine. Nida'ul Islam is a bimonthly magazine produced by the Islamic Youth Movement in Sydney, Australia.

As you read, consider the following questions:

1. What is the "Middle East Order," according to the magazine?
2. In the view of the magazine, why do the Zionists want to establish local authority in Palestine under the leadership of Yasir Arafat?
3. According to a 1935 fatwa [religious ruling] cited by Nida'ul Islam, how should Muslims who sell their land in Palestine to Jews be punished?

Reprinted from "Palestine: History, Case, and Solution," editorial, Nida'ul Islam, January/February 1996, by permission of Nida'ul Islam magazine.

[The Jews] with their support from the Christian countries ... [transformed] their dream of occupying Palestine into a reality in 1948 after some wars in which the Arabic regimes played the biggest role in weaving the defeat and attempting to demolish the will to resist the schemes of the Jews in the holy land of Sham.

The Zionist scheme to dominate the Muslim world reached various stages of development for many reasons some of which:

1. The Zionist domination of the ruling centres in most of the world capitals.

2. The Zionist domination of the spheres of economics, money, and media in the capitals of the Christian West.

3. Recruiting Arabic rulers whose mission is the fulfillment of the plans of the Jews with all sincerity.

4. Working through a strategy with certain stages at the creation of the nation of the children of Zion and up to future centuries. This strategy was translated into the peace missions which forced into submission the regimes of the Arabic resistance.

[Former Egyptian president Anwar] Sadat started on this road in an open manner when he visited AlQuds and signed the Camp David accord [a peace agreement between Egypt and Israel]. This opened the way for the children of Zion to dominate Egyptian markets economically, culturally, and through the media. He was followed in this policy by Yaser Arafat who imposed himself onto the leadership of the Palestine Liberation Organization (PLO). Arafat was in turn followed by the Hashimite devil Husain [the king of Jordan] through his signing of the last peace treaty with Israel. These will be followed in the near future with peace treaties with Syria and Lebanon (May Allah forbid this).

All this comes through a thorough scheme called the Middle East Order where Israel will sit comfortably on its throne and rule over the Arab and Islamic world at the various economic, political, and information levels until it achieves its dream of establishing the government of the greater Israel. This will make it easier for Israel to kill the spirit of resistance in the Muslim people and then convince them that Israel has appeared in the region to remain.

ZIONISM'S GOALS

These enemies have realised that the strength of this Ummah [community] lies in its Islam. For this reason they have worked from the beginning to remove the creed aspect from the conscience of the Ummah, at one time by placing evil rulers who smite the forerunners of the revival which are embodied in the

Islamic movements and at other times by inciting the Western world against Islam and its Jihad movements through the tunes of fundamentalism and terrorism.

They also worked at the same time to domesticate the Palestinian people through the utilisation of the latest method of terrorism, oppression, and starvation to break the bone of resistance which came to the forefront alive with the blessed Islamic Intifada.

However, have they been able to achieve this?

It is true that the apostate Arabic regimes have signed—and will sign—the "peace" treaties.

It is also true that these regimes are competing to earn the pleasure of the New American World Order, which is sponsoring 'Israel' as a ruler over the region.

It is also true that the operation of official recognition has begun hand and foot in many Arabic and Islamic countries, through changing the education curricula, the opening of the markets to Israeli products and the establishment of seminars and conferences etc.

PLANS ARE DOOMED TO FAIL

However, all these plans have forgotten that the people are Islamic, and that this Giant has awakened and risen from its rest. These are its Mujahid [people who wage jihad] heralds shuddering the earth under the feet of the despots in all areas of the Muslim Ummah, and these are able after relying on Allah The Exalted to bring defeat to their enemies.

These are the plans of Israel to make everything acceptable continuing in Egypt since the 1980s. It has not been able to reach more than a few of the agents of the regime who have sold their religion whilst the vast majority of people continue to reject Israel, not changing their views towards it as an occupying enemy which has usurped Muslim lands in Sham.

Nothing has been written for the latest plans of gaining acceptance except failure. Because the Muslim people reject that tyrant country, their apostate regimes are not able to change that view despite their intricate schemes.

The will of Jihad in our Ummah will continue to the day of judgement. This is confirmed by the noble authentic ahadith [the customs and traditions of Muhammad and his companions], particularly in the blessed land of Sham.

However, this does not mean in any way that we must reside in that land and await victory—victory does not come without struggle and sacrifice.

The situation which our Ummah is currently going through is regarded as the most important and most dangerous of stages. It witnesses the resurgence of Islam accompanied with the biggest rejectionist plot against the people of this blessed resurgence which aims at the ending of the Islamic Jihad movements and replacing them with an Islam which has Western meaning and content.

The plots of the children of Zion in Palestine aim at wiping the Muslim identity and replacing this with a comical local authority under the leadership of Yaser Arafat. This authority will work to achieve the rest of their plans and relieve them of the hardship of keeping peace in the Palestinian camps which form a foreboding security nightmare for their soldiers.

Jihad Is the Answer

Here in reality is what the personal authority of Arafat attempts to establish by pursuing the Mujahideen, imprisoning them, and torturing them.

The time has come for the Islamic movement to realise that the only way out lies in Jihad in the cause of Allah for the liberation of land and people and the establishment of the religion of Allah, and every other path will lead to complete failure without doubt. They must also realise that alternate attempts by the Islamic movements are doomed to failure. They must be weary of election trap regardless of its nature, and must continue with resistance in all its forms.

Victory is coming without doubt regardless of the variety of schemes, because this is a promise from Allah Most High: "So if the promise of the second came to pass, they will disgrace your faces, and they will enter the mosque as they entered it the first time and they may destroy what they overcome with complete destruction."

Illegal Land Sales

The Ummah is unanimous about the illegality of reconciliation with the Jews who have usurped the land of Palestine. The trusted scholars have also decreed that whoever sells his land to the Jews or whoever accepts reconciliation with them knowing the harm of this to the Muslims is an apostate who has rejected Islam.

After the fall of the 'Uthmany Caliphate [the ruler of the Ottoman Empire, which fell at the end of World War I], the scholars of Palestine realised the size and danger of the plot which had been weaved, and the designs of the Jews to their land. So they gathered on 26 January 1935 in the Alaqsa mosque in the holy land and issued a Fatwa [religious ruling], the most important part of which states: "*further, we the issuers of the Fatwa ... after research and looking into what would arise from the sale of the land in Palestine to the Jews, with looking into the intents of the Zionists to Turn this holy Muslim land into Jewish land, taking it from the hands of its inhabitants and keeping them away from it....*

"*After looking at the fatwas which have been issued by the Muslim scholars in Iraq, Egypt, India, Morocco, Syria, Palestine, and other Muslim countries, which have unanimously agreed to the illegality of the sale of Palestinian land to the Jews, as well as broking or facilitating in any way or mean the sale of any land to the Jews, and the illegality of accepting this and keeping quiet over it. Further, all this has become with respect to each Palestinian knowing of the result and accepting it an act of apostasy and rejection of Islam....*"

PEACE PROPOSALS ARE THE WRONG SOLUTION

[Peace] initiatives, the so-called peaceful solutions, and the international conferences to resolve the Palestinian problem, are all contrary to the beliefs of the Islamic Resistance Movement. For renouncing any part of Palestine means renouncing part of the religion; the nationalism of the Islamic Resistance Movement is part of its faith, the movement educates its members to adhere to its principles and to raise the banner of Allah over their homeland as they fight their Jihad: "Allah is the all-powerful, but most people are not aware."...

There is no solution to the Palestinian problem except by Jihad. The initiatives, proposals and International Conferences are but a waste of time, an exercise in futility. The Palestinian people are too noble to have their future, their right and their destiny submitted to a vain game.

Article Thirteen of the Charter of the Hamas. Found at http://www.womeningreen.org/hamas.htm.

Then the scholars mentioned the various corruptions which arise from the sale of land to the Jews with respect to the expulsion of Muslims from their homes and the stopping the mention of The Name of Allah in His mosques, and befriending the Jews and supporting them against the Muslims and the betrayal of Allah and His Messenger. "*So let it be known from all that we have put forward of reasons, results, statements, rulings, and fatwas that the one who sells his land in Palestine to the Jews, whether directly or through an agent, and the agent in this sale and the one who facilitates it and the one who assists in it in any manner knowing of the aforementioned results, each of those is not to be prayed over nor buried in the Muslim graves. They must also be ostracised and boycotted, as well as degrading them and abstaining from compassion towards* them or coming near them whether they are fathers, children, brothers, or spouses. . . . Further, silence with respect to the deeds of these, and acquiescing to them is strictly forbidden."

This accord was signed by two hundred and forty nine (249) scholars overall. It is a Fatwa declaring illegal to forego any part of Palestine.

On 29 November 1947 the scholars of Alazhar issued a call after the resolution of the United Nations to divide Palestine into two countries, a Jewish and a Palestinian. This call included: "The resolution of the United Nations is a resolution from a body without authority. It is an oppressive, and transgressing resolution which has no justice or equity." Then the Muslim scholars called for Jihad to liberate Palestine: "Block their path, and sit for them in every vantage point, boycott them with respect to their trade and do not deal with them, and prepare the requisites of Jihad amongst yourselves. . . . Fulfill what Allah has required of you. . . ."

TREATIES WITH ISRAEL ARE ILLEGAL

Then occurred the various treasons by the puppet Arabic governments which pursued the Mujahideen groups and stopped them from fighting against the Jews, and the country of Israel was established on the land of Palestine. Then in 1956 a committee of the scholars of Alazhar issued a Fatwa forbidding a truce with the new Jewish government which declared the truce with Israel—and those who incite to it—"to be not permitted by law because of what it contains of acquiescing to the transgressor and allowing him to continue to usurp and entrench itself in the land. . . . So it is not permitted for the Muslims to reconcile with these Jews who have usurped the land of Palestine and transgressed against its people and their wealth in any manner whatsoever which will allow the Jews to remain on these holy Islamic lands as a nation. In fact, it is required of them to cooperate together with their varied tongues and colours and ethnicity to return this country to its people, and to protect the Alaqsa mosque . . . and to exert all they can to cleanse the land of the country from any trace of these transgressors. Whoever falls short in this or neglects it or discourages the Muslims from it or calls to whatever leads to the dispersion of the word and Muslims, and assists the colonialists and Zionists to fulfill their plans against the Arabs and the Muslims and against the Arabic and Islamic country is—according to the law of Islam—one who left the Muslims and committed the gravest of sins."

The Imam of Alazhar Hasan Ma'moun issued the following Fatwa: "Palestine is a land liberated by the Muslims who have lived therein for a long time, so it has become a part of the Islamic countries, most of its inhabitants are Muslims, there resides amongst them a minority of other religions, so it is a Muslim country wherein Muslim law applies". . . and added "The attack of the enemy against a Muslim country is not accepted under Islamic law regardless of its reasons and motives. The land of Islam must remain in the hand of its people. . . . What is required of the Muslims in the situation of transgression against any Islamic country—and there is no distinction amongst Muslims—is Jihad against the enemy with force, and this is an individual obligation upon all its people . . . so when all the Muslim countries are regarded as a home for every Muslim, the duty of Jihad forms an obligation upon its people first, and upon other Muslims who live in other countries second."

LIBERATING PALESTINE

A Fatwa which has issued in this matter is the one which had been signed by sixty-three scholars and thinkers from eighteen countries, this is some of what came in it: "We declare with what Allah has taken upon us of oath to reveal the truth that Jihad is the only path to liberate Palestine, and that it is not permitted in any situation to acknowledge one hand span of Palestinian land for the Jews. It does not fall on any person or group to acknowledge a right for the Jews to Palestine or to forego to them any part thereof or thereto.

Such an acknowledgment would be treason to Allah and the messenger and the trust which all Muslims have been trusted to guard, Allah says: "O those who have believed, do not betray Allah and the messenger, and do not betray your trusts whilst you are knowing." What treason is bigger than the sale of the sanctities of the Muslims and the forfeiture of the Muslim countries to the enemies of Allah and His messenger and the believers?

We stress that Palestine is Muslim land and will remain so and it will be liberated by the champions of Islam from the filth of the Jews as it had been liberated by Salahuddin from the filth of the crusaders, and you will hear of this after some time.". . .

From the aforementioned, it becomes clear to us without doubt or argument, that truce with the country of Israel is a matter which is not permitted by law regardless of what the claimants and the whisperers claim and whisper. Jihad with iron and fire is the only way to reclaim Palestine from the hands of the Jews and to return it to the rule of Islam. Whoever amongst the Muslims permits a truce with the Jews, and acquiesces to the establishment of their country knowing of the illegality of this will be regarded as an apostate, and shall be treated as such.

"The mask of religion, ... must be torn from [the extremists'] face and they should be recognized for what they stand for, greed and power."

THE ISLAMIC FAITH DOES NOT CONDONE TERRORISM

Seifeldin Ashmawy

In the following viewpoint, Seifeldin Ashmawy contends that Islam does not condone or justify acts of terrorism. He asserts that Islamic extremists such as Hamas and American Muslim organizations that support Hamas do not represent the authentic Muslim view. These extremists pose a threat to the Middle East peace process and to the United States and should be prevented from carrying out attacks, Ashmawy claims. Ashmawy was the president of the Peace Press Association, a moderate Muslim organization. He died in a car accident in January 1998.

As you read, consider the following questions:

1. According to Ashmawy, what does "jihad" mean?
2. In the view of the author, how did Hamas rise to power in Palestine?
3. How are U.S. policies concerning terrorism contradictory, according to Ashmawy?

Excerpted from Seifeldin Ashmawy's testimony before the U.S. Senate, Committee on Foreign Affairs, Subcommittee on Near East and South Asian Affairs, March 19, 1996.

DEFINITIONS

Terrorism. Although the United Nations Charter grants people the right to carry arms to defend themselves and their land, when an individual or group of people attack, kill and destroy civilians and their properties this act departs from being a freedom fighter to become a terrorist.

Extremism. When someone who believes in a religion and tries to live and act according to the literal interpretation of certain verses in his holy book without adhering to the moral codes of the religion he becomes an extremist. The extremist adheres to the ritual rather than the tenets of the faith.

Jihad in Islam. Jihad is an Arabic word meaning strive. The main jihad in Islam is spiritual, encouraging people to strive to overcome the lower desires of man.

The physical jihad which is erroneously translated as "holy war" was imposed on the early converts of Islam to permit them to defend themselves against the aggression of the pagans.

The Koran, the Holy Book of the Muslims, stipulates that this physical struggle should be only in self defense.

INACCURATE INTERPRETATIONS

Sharia. Sharia, known and translated as Islamic law, is not a codified law revealed to the Muslims. It is a group of interpretations and guides of some Muslim scholars. These interpretations are not absolute, although the extremists are attempting to claim them as if they were revealed from God.

Islamic Government. There is no such thing mentioned in the Koran or described by the Prophet of Islam. There was no specific direction or specifications in the Koran or stated by the Prophet about who would lead the Muslim community.

The first leader after the Prophet was duly elected by the community. After his election, Abu Bakre said to the people, "I am not the best of you. If I lead you on the right path help me; and if I stray correct me." It is obvious from this quotation that this was a leader elected by the people without any religious appointment. The extremists are calling for a theocratic government, giving the leader of the government absolute power and rule.

Sunni. It is a description applied to the Muslims majority, "1 billion 400 million" who adhere to the teachings of the Koran and the Prophet.

Shiites. It is an Arabic word meaning party. Its complete name is "Party of Ali," the fourth ruler of the Muslim community, and first cousin of the Prophet. He was killed by some people who seceded from his camp. The Shiites promote the idea that the only rightful leader of the Muslim community should be from Ali's descendants. They call this descendant "Imam." This leader has absolute religious and civil power over all his followers.

The current Shiite leader is infallible and reigns with the same absolute powers until the descendant of Ali appears.

A CHANGING COMMUNITY

My name is Seif Ashmawy, I am a Sunni Muslim and an American citizen. I migrated from Egypt in 1969. In the past quarter of a century I have seen a huge change in my Muslim community.

Unfortunately, most of our institutions in the United States are controlled by either extremists or profiteers. Both are abusing the freedom which we enjoy and furthermore, they are being supported and financed by the closest allies of the United States, the Saudis, Kuwaitis and the Gulf States.

I know that by appearing before you, I am placing my life, as well as that of my family in jeopardy; since I will be accused by the extremists as a traitor to Islam. However I have chosen my path, willingly, to explain to Muslims and non-Muslims, the authentic Islam, which loves and respects the life of every human being. I am here to defend and protect my country, the United States of America and to defend my religion, Islam.

ASHMAWY'S ACCOMPLISHMENTS

I have studied my religion and others extensively but not academically. I have been doing this work actively, giving lectures in synagogues, churches and universities about Islam and trying to reverse the ideologies of the extremists.

I organized a group of intellectual Muslims, who believe in moderation and authentic Islam, called Peace Press Association, a New Jersey Corporation. Under the auspices of this organization we publish a monthly newspaper called The Voice of Peace, distributed in 10 states.

I appear monthly on WABC Radio program, Religion On The Line, representing the moderate voice of Islam, reaching over 112 million listeners.

In 1992, prior to any implementation of a peace between the Palestine Liberation Organization (PLO), Jordan, and Israel, I went on a mission for peace to the Middle East with an inter-religious group, meeting political leaders in Egypt, Jordan, Syria, West Bank, and Israel and reached out to the common citizen in each country, explaining to them the importance of peace to all of us.

It is important to emphasize that all of these efforts are being made without any support from any country or political or religious organizations. Therefore, I can assure you that my views are totally independent.

TERRORISM DOES NOT HAVE RELIGIOUS JUSTIFICATION

On many occasions I have publicly denounced terrorism and extremism in any form, political or religious. It is my opinion that crossing the line to kill civilians is departing from ethnic and religious morals. The mask of religion, which the extremists wear, must be torn from their face and they should be recognized for what they stand for, greed and power. It is my opinion that the extremists among Muslims are not motivated by religion but by their own political agenda. I denounce the acts of Hamas since their purpose is to destroy the peace process and to hurt the national identity of the Palestinians. In the same token I denounce the collective punishment carried out by the Israeli Government. Israel failed to help improve the social, economic and political lives of the Palestinians in the occupied territories. Allowing Hamas to fill the vacancy; giving them more credibility and power to recruit members from among the dissatisfied and disillusioned young people.

It is my opinion that the United States has a moral obligation to fight extremism and terrorism; and should not place the bur-

den on the governments of Egypt, Algeria, Israel and Palestinian Authority.

I was very disappointed when the Congress failed to pass the Terrorist Bill disregarding the Americans' safety and interest. I am disappointed with the White House in its attempt to bridge with Muslims. They have courted extremists such as AMC rather than reaching out for the moderate. [In April 1996, the Comprehensive Terrorism Prevention Act of 1995 was signed into law.]

The American Muslim Council is an umbrella group of the "Muslim Brotherhood" and it is actively involved in championing the movements of Hamas, Algerian Islamic Salvation Front (FIS), Tunisian Al-Nahda movement, Turkish Welfare Party, Jordanian Islamic Action Front and the Sudanese National Islamic Front. The American Muslim Council does not represent American Muslims; it represents the extremists and those that believe in terrorism.

A THREATENED PEACE PROCESS

It cannot be emphasized enough that the peace process in the Middle East is essential not only for the area but for the whole world. And the peace process is in danger as long as terrorists have the upper hand and terrorism is uncurbed.

What has taken place in [early 1996] in Israel reflects the determination and desperation of the extremists to destroy the peace process and achieve political power.

The extremists on both sides, Palestinian and Israeli, have the same objective; and both are short-sighted.

Since the signing of the peace treaty between Egypt and Israel in 1978, the wars between the Arabs and Israelis have ended. The Arabs realized that there could be no war without Egypt. However, Egypt suffered greatly after signing the Camp David Accord. At the same time the Palestinians who had placed their hope in Egypt's power to win their country back also lost their hope to achieve a just peace.

In this hopeless situation, the United States and Israel did not grasp the opportunity to improve the political, social and economic life of the Palestinians in the occupied territories. The desperation of the people evolved into the uprising known as the Intifada, in 1987.

HAMAS IS DANGEROUS

The political vacuum of the situation created Hamas. Hamas established clinics and schools throughout the occupied territories. As a result, these areas became the breeding ground and the areas to recruit membership for Hamas.

In the atmosphere of poverty, desperation and loss of identity people turn to the only thing that gives them solace, religion; and unfortunately, to its extreme form. Hamas recognized this and grasped the opportunity to achieve a political advantage, calling for an "Islamic State."

The policy makers of the United States seem unaware that the victory of Hamas will cause additional problems in the area. With the extremists in power a religious problem will arise between the Muslims and Christians. This problem will then spread to Israel, Syria, Jordan and other parts of the Middle East.

In the fight against international terrorism, we cannot expect Yasir Arafat and [then-Israeli prime minister] Shimon Peres to do it alone. Which is why the involvement of the U.S. is so important. To that end, the commitment of American resources to stop extremists from carrying out their deadly war against civilians is absolutely vital. But the battle against terrorism and extremism cannot be contained to the borders of the Middle East. There must be a concerted effort to defeat the forces of extremism; and simultaneously support moderates in their battle against the radicals no matter where they are. In this matter, I must tell you that I have personally been involved with fighting the extremists.

In my community in New Jersey, I was involved in confronting Sheik Omar Abdul Rahman before the World Trade Center bombing. I debated the Sheik and his followers. I have tracked and seen the rise of extremists elsewhere in the United States during the past decade.

Indeed, what I have discovered is that the heart, if not the soul, of the extremists—is in fact largely in the United States, where these radicals have set up many of their fundraising and political headquarters. These groups have literally hijacked the mainstream Islamic organizations here in the United States. They are the engines that drive the radical groups in the Middle East. Besides millions of dollars of funds as well as propaganda, these groups do something far more dangerous: they provide legitimacy to the radicals.

OBJECTIVES OF HAMAS

Hamas' objective is to destroy the ongoing peace process between the Palestinian Authority, represented by Yasir Arafat, and Israel. They believe that by changing the public opinion of the Israeli majority who want peace they will destroy the opportunity for peace as well as Arafat. If Hamas achieves these goals then the Palestinian people will return to their desperation and extremism will have won, giving rise to greater bloodshed and more wars. . . .

The U.S. policies appear to be contradictory, looking for short-term solutions rather than long term.

We have buried our heads in the sand believing that terrorism like the devastation of the two World Wars would never land on our shores. However, the World Trade Center explosions followed by the bombing in Oklahoma has proven us wrong. The neglect by Congress to take serious measures to curb the influence of extremism and protect the American society from future terrorism is astonishing. The success of the extremists in the Middle East will allow them to export their ideology and tactics to the American soil. Their slogan, "The U.S.A. is the Great Satan," will motivate them to destroy the culture and fabric of the American society.

It is imperative that the U.S. policy abroad be strong and vigorous to help eradicate extremism in its own land before the extremists export it to ours. I am here to tell you that there is a serious problem in the United States. You need to ensure not only that terrorists are confronted in the Middle East but here in the U.S. as well. The problem is no longer a geographical battle. The future of the real and true Islam—a moderate Islam—is at stake. And you as members of the U.S. Senate have an obligation to root out the extremists and provide support to the genuine moderates.

PERIODICAL BIBLIOGRAPHY

The following articles have been selected to supplement the diverse views presented in this chapter. Addresses are provided for periodicals not indexed in the *Readers' Guide to Periodical Literature*, the *Alternative Press Index*, the *Social Sciences Index*, or the *Index to Legal Periodicals and Books*.

Tom Barrett	"Racist Terror in Oklahoma," *International Viewpoint*, June 1995.
Robert James Bidinotto	"Beyond the Pale," *Freeman*, July 1995. Available from the Foundation for Economic Education, Irvington-on-Hudson, NY 10533.
Azmi Bishara	"Where Suicide Bombs Come From," *New York Times*, February 17, 1995.
Gloria Borger	"Debasing the Political Currency," *U.S. News & World Report*, May 8, 1995.
Barbara Dority	"Is the Extremist Right Entirely Wrong?" *Humanist*, November/December 1995.
William Dowell	"Defending Islam," *Time*, October 9, 1995.
Plemon T. El-Amin	"A Muslim Voice Against Terrorism," *Tikkun*, March/April 1995.
Samuel Francis	"Principalities and Powers," *Chronicles*, August 1995. Available from the Rockford Institute, 928 N. Main St., Rockford, IL 61103.
Wanda Franz	"Violence Is Not Pro-Life," *National Right to Life News*, January 1995. Available from 419 7th St. NW, Suite 500, Washington, DC 20004.
New York Times	"Excerpts from Manuscript Linked to Suspect in Seventeen-Year Series of Bombings," August 2, 1995.
Josh Passell	"New Patriot Games," *Index on Censorship*, September/October 1995.
Carla Anne Robbins and Hugh Pope	"Bombings Put Focus on Saudi Patron of Terror," *Wall Street Journal*, August 10, 1998.
Kirkpatrick Sale	"Toward a Portrait of the Unabomber," *New York Times*, August 6, 1995.
Dave Skinner	"In Defense of the Militia," *USA Today*, July 1996.
Amanda Swarr	"Terrorism and Murder: The True Intent of the 'Pro-Life' Movement Exposed," *Off Our Backs*, May 1995.

CHAPTER 4

HOW SHOULD THE UNITED STATES RESPOND TO TERRORISM?

Chapter Preface

In February 1976, President Ford signed Executive Order 12333, which stated "no person employed by or acting on behalf of the United States government shall engage in, or conspire to engage in, assassination." This order followed the discovery that the Central Intelligence Agency (CIA) had unsuccessfully attempted to assassinate Cuban president Fidel Castro and other persons perceived to be threats to national security. More than two decades later, debate has been raised as to whether Executive Order 12333 should be circumvented, in light of the actions of terrorists such as Osama Bin Ladin, the alleged mastermind behind the August 1998 bombings of U.S. embassies in Kenya and Tanzania. Some analysts argue that assassinating Bin Ladin and other terrorist leaders is justifiable, while others contend that assassinations are immoral and could potentially lead to further attacks against the United States.

Those who support government-sponsored assassination claim that it is an effective way to deter terrorists without threatening civilians. Edward G. Shirley, who once worked as a Middle Eastern–targets officer for the CIA, writes in the *Wall Street Journal*: "Common sense dictates that in the war against terrorism—against those who are killing Americans—the U.S. must be willing to kill terrorist chiefs." People who favor this solution also note that the current U.S. policy, such as bombing terrorist camps and factories, causes significant casualties and damage and could create a greater risk of retribution. In an editorial, the *New Republic* states: "If we continue to target areas rather than individuals, we risk creating even more genuinely aggrieved people . . . who will be available as new recruits for terrorist groups."

However, other analysts assert that the United States must continue to respect the executive order. They argue that the threat of retaliation would actually be greater if assassinations became acceptable because killing terrorist leaders ensures their martyrdom, thereby rallying others to their cause. These observers also maintain that opting for assassination would weaken the United States' moral standing in the world. According to an editorial in *Newsday*, "Dispatching death squads to kill political enemies, believed to be criminals but convicted of no crimes, would be about as un-American as it gets."

While assassination remains an especially controversial response to terrorism, the United States has implemented other solutions. In the following chapter, the authors debate which responses to terrorism are most effective.

> "Although no system can guarantee full protection against the threat of terrorist activities, [aviation] security improvements can help to reduce that threat."

TOUGHER AVIATION SECURITY MEASURES WILL HELP REDUCE TERRORISM

Keith O. Fultz

In the following viewpoint, Keith O. Fultz contends that, while aviation security has gotten better, further steps are necessary in order to reduce terrorism. He explains that certain improvements, such as new systems to screen passengers and match bags to passengers, have not been fully implemented due to high costs and construction delays. Fultz argues that the Federal Aviation Administration (FAA) must continue to strengthen airport security in order to reduce the threat of terrorism as much as possible. Fultz is an assistant comptroller general in the General Accounting Office.

As you read, consider the following questions:

1. Why is automated passenger profiling not discriminatory, according to Fultz?
2. In the author's view, who is the best line of defense in airport security?
3. According to the author, what are the parallels between the responses to the crashes of Pam Am Flight 103 and TWA Flight 800?

Excerpted from "Status of Aviation Security Efforts with a Focus on the National Safe Skies Alliance and Passenger Profiling Criteria," Keith O. Fultz's testimony before the U.S. House of Representatives Committee on Transportation and Infrastructure, Subcommittee on Aviation, May 14, 1998.

We commend the Chairman for holding these hearings on aviation security. Improving the security of our nation's aviation system is an extremely important national issue, and we believe aggressive and strong congressional vigilance will be needed to maintain the momentum for improving the system. For this reason, we appreciate the opportunity to testify on what progress has been made and what remains to be done. As the events over the last several years have made us all aware, the threat of terrorism against the United States has increased. Aviation is, and will remain, an attractive target for terrorists, so protecting civil aviation continues to be an urgent national issue. . . .

Currently, the Federal Aviation Administration (FAA), other federal agencies, and the aviation industry are implementing a number of recommendations made by the Commission. Some of these recommendations are similar to legislative mandates the Congress enacted under the Federal Aviation Reauthorization Act of 1996, and FAA is also addressing them. (We will refer to these recommendations and mandates as initiatives.) Our testimony focuses on our recent review of the implementation of the key initiatives. . . .

EVALUATING THE FAA'S EFFORTS

Providing effective security is a complex and difficult task because of the size of the U.S. aviation system, the differences among airlines and airports, and the unpredictable nature of terrorism. FAA was attempting to build consensus with the aviation community on how to improve aviation security when, in 1996, TWA Flight 800 crashed. Because the crash was initially suspected to be a terrorist act, national attention focused on the need to address aviation security vulnerabilities. The President created a Commission to review aviation safety and security issues, and the Congress held hearings. The Commission made a total of 31 recommendations for improving aviation security at our nation's airports. In the 1996 Reauthorization Act, the Congress mandated that FAA take several actions to improve aviation security, and the Congress provided $144.2 million in the Omnibus Consolidated Appropriations Act of 1997 to purchase commercially available advanced security equipment for screening checked and carry-on baggage and to conduct related activities.

As we reported in April 1998, FAA has made progress in a number of critical areas to improve aviation security as recommended by the Commission and mandated by the Reauthorization Act. However, the agency has experienced delays of up to 12 months in completing the five efforts we reviewed: passenger profiling, explosives detection technologies, passenger-bag matching, vulnerability assessments, and the certification of screening companies and the performance of security screeners. FAA officials said many of the expected completion dates were ambitious, and they have extended them to take into account the complexities and time-consuming activities involved. We found that delays were caused by the new and relatively untested technologies, limited funds, and problems with equipment installation and contractors' performance. In some cases, FAA must develop regulations to establish new requirements. Airports, air carriers, and screening companies then must establish programs to meet those requirements. Based on FAA's current schedule and milestones, this whole process for enhancing the nation's aviation security system will take years to fully implement.

I will briefly discuss the status of these five initiatives and the actions that FAA and others need to take before they can be fully implemented.

SCREENING PASSENGERS AND BAGGAGE

Automated passenger profiling is a computer-based method that permits air carriers to focus on the small percentage of passengers who may pose security risks and whose bags should be screened by explosives detection equipment or matched with the boarding passengers. The system developed to screen passengers is known as the computer-assisted passenger screening (CAPS) system. It is designed to enable air carriers to more quickly separate passengers into two categories—those who do not require additional security attention and those who do. None of the major carriers had an automated system in place by December 31, 1997, as FAA originally planned. However, as of February 1998, three major air carriers had voluntarily implemented the system, and all but one major carrier are expected to have voluntarily implemented it by September 1998. [As of February 1999, all seven major airlines were using the CAPS system.]

Concerns have been raised about the potential of this system to function in a discriminatory manner. However, the Department of Justice has determined that the screening process used by the system does not discriminate against travelers because it does not record or give any consideration to the race, color, national or ethnic origin, religion, or gender of passengers. Nor does it include as a screening factor any passenger traits, such as a passenger's name or mode of dress, that may be directly associated with discriminatory judgments. To ensure the system is run in a nondiscriminatory manner, the system will be reviewed periodically by FAA and the Department of Justice.

Explosives detection technologies are screening devices that have the capability to detect the potential existence of explosives that can be concealed in carry-on or checked baggage. This area is one that recently has seen a substantial increase in funding. FAA is a year behind schedule in deploying this equipment. These delays have been caused, in part, by the inexperience of the contractor hired to install the equipment and the ongoing or planned construction projects that must be completed before the equipment can be installed at certain airports. By December 1997, FAA originally planned to deploy 54 certified explosives detection systems to screen checked bags and 489 trace detection devices to screen passengers' carry-on bags at major airports. However, as of the end of April 1998, FAA had deployed only 21 of the certified explosives detection systems and only about 250 of the trace detection devices. FAA now plans to have all of them installed and operational by December 1998. At that time, still only a limited number of airports and a fraction of the flying public would be covered. [As of February 1999, 74 explosive detection systems and more than 300 trace detection devices had been installed. The

FAA will eventually be able to cover 76 major airports which handle more than 90 percent of the flying public.]

During the deployment of this equipment, FAA plans to gather information and evaluate how well the equipment is working in the field. This is important because we previously reported that there were significant differences between how these certified systems performed in the field and in the laboratory. Both the cost of the equipment—two units in one place costing about $2 million are required to meet FAA's certification standard—and the speed at which the equipment can screen bags have been concerns to the aviation industry. FAA is interested in identifying and certifying less expensive and faster equipment and has continued to fund research to develop more equipment that could potentially meet FAA's certification standard.

Matching checked bags to the passengers who actually board a flight allows airlines to reduce the risk from concealed explosives because they can remove the bags of people who do not board the aircraft. According to FAA, when passenger-bag matching is fully implemented, the system will match some passengers, who are either randomly selected or who have been identified through the profiling system, with their bags. FAA began examining the feasibility of matching bags with passengers before the Commission's final report was issued and the Reauthorization Act was passed. In June 1997, the agency completed a pilot program at selected airports. Although FAA was required by the Reauthorization Act to report to the Congress on the pilot program within 30 days after its completion, it did not do so. In the fall of 1997, FAA notified the Congress that the report would be delayed because FAA had agreed with the airline industry to combine this report with an economic analysis of the impact of matching passengers and bags systemwide. Some air carriers have already voluntarily begun to match some passengers and bags for their domestic flights. In November 1998, FAA expects to issue a regulation that will require air carriers to implement such a program within 30 days—about 1 year later than the Commission expected.

AIRPORT VULNERABILITIES MUST BE ASSESSED

In both the Reauthorization Act and the Commission's final report, FAA was directed to conduct a number of vulnerability assessments in an airport environment to identify weaknesses in security measures that could allow threats to be successfully carried out. In August 1996, recognizing the vital role of vulnerability assessments, we recommended that steps be taken to conduct a comprehensive review of the safety and security of all major airports and air carriers to identify the strengths and weaknesses of their procedures to protect the flying public and to identify vulnerabilities in the system. FAA has three separate efforts under way.

First, FAA is developing a standardized model for conducting airport vulnerability assessments, as the Commission recommended. FAA is working with several companies that are using different models for assessing the vulnerabilities at 14 major airports. FAA has established a panel to review the assessment results and to select the best model for assessing a facility's vulnerabilities. The agency plans to make this model available to airlines and airports in March 1999. Although some delays have occurred in starting the assessments, they have not been significant.

Second, to address the Reauthorization Act's requirement for FAA and the Federal Bureau of Investigation (FBI) to jointly assess threats and vulnerabilities at high-risk airports, FAA and FBI officials conducted their first assessment in December 1997. In February 1998, FAA officials said they would begin conducting one to two assessments each month. The results of the joint assessments will be used for comparing threats and vulnerabilities at different airports. By having both threat and vulnerability information, FAA and FBI officials should be able to determine which airports and which areas of airports present the highest risks. FAA and FBI have agreed to a schedule for assessing 31 airports considered to be high-risk candidates by the end of calendar year 1999. The Reauthorization Act, however, called for the initial assessments to be completed by October 9, 1999. The schedule FAA and FBI agreed to calls for their reviews at 28 of the 31 airports to be completed by this date.

Third, the Reauthorization Act mandates that FAA require airports and air carriers to conduct periodic vulnerability assessments. FAA plans to require that airports and air carriers incorporate periodic assessments into their individual security programs. However, FAA stated that before implementing this change, it intends to make the standardized model that it is developing available to both airports and air carriers for use in conducting these assessments. As mentioned previously, FAA expects the model to be available in March 1999. Implementation of the periodic assessments is to begin around mid-1999.

SECURITY EMPLOYEES SHOULD BE TRAINED

Both the Reauthorization Act and the Commission's report directed FAA to certify the screening companies that air carriers contract with to provide security at airport checkpoints and to improve the training of the personnel doing the screening. Certifying the companies would ensure that these companies and their employees meet established standards and have consistent qualifications. FAA plans to complete the final regulation for certifying screening companies and screener performance in March 2000. According to FAA officials, they need time to develop performance standards based on screener performance data and to incorporate those standards into the final regulation.

Improving the training and testing of people hired by these companies to screen passengers' baggage at airport security checkpoints would also improve aviation security. Regardless of advances in technology, the people who operate the equipment are the last and best line of defense against the introduction of any dangerous object into the aviation system. Currently, the people who are hired to screen baggage attend a standardized classroom training program. FAA is deploying a computerized, self-paced training and testing system, called the Screener Proficiency Evaluation and Reporting System (SPEARS). This effort was begun well before the Commission issued its initial report and the Reauthorization Act was enacted. As of February 1998, FAA had deployed computer-based training systems for personnel who use X-ray machines for screening carry-on bags at 17 major airports. Deployment is planned for two additional major airports by May 1998. FAA had also awarded a contract to deploy these systems at another 60 airports, but as of March 1998, the agency had decided to deploy only 15 of the 60 systems because it lacked necessary funding. If funds are available, FAA plans to deploy the other 45 systems by the end of fiscal year 1998 or early fiscal year 1999. [By December 1998, 79 airports had computer-based training.]

FURTHER SECURITY IMPROVEMENTS ARE NECESSARY

Although no system can guarantee full protection against the threat of terrorist activities, security improvements can help to reduce that threat. Further improvements in the nation's aviation security system will need long-term efforts by FAA and the aviation industry. . . .

In closing, . . . vulnerabilities in our aviation security system still exist. While FAA has made some progress in addressing these vulnerabilities, it is crucial that the Congress maintain vigilant oversight of the agency's efforts. When we testified before several committees following the crash of TWA Flight 800, a parallel was drawn between actions taken following Pan Am

Flight 103 and TWA Flight 800. In both instances, presidential commissions were formed, vulnerabilities were identified, and a period of heightened activity by the government, the aviation industry, and the media ensued. Regrettably, after the commission investigating Pan Am Flight 103 issued its report, activity began to wane and not much progress was made. Although improvements have been made since the crash of TWA Flight 800, we must ensure that momentum will not be lost.

"The threat of airline terrorism cannot be eliminated unless air travel is banned."

TOUGHER AVIATION SECURITY MEASURES WILL NOT REDUCE TERRORISM

Robert W. Hahn

Aviation security measures are costly and ineffective, argues Robert W. Hahn in the following viewpoint. According to Hahn, the plan issued by the White House Commission on Aviation Safety and Security in September 1996 is flawed. Hahn maintains that these proposals—including baggage screening and passenger profiling—will increase travel delays. In addition, he asserts, such procedures will be expensive and save few lives, because the policies will not have a significant impact on the behavior of terrorists. Hahn is a resident scholar at the American Enterprise Institute, a public policy organization that researches government and private enterprise issues.

As you read, consider the following questions:

1. What delay cost cannot be quantified easily, in Hahn's view?
2. As cited by the author, what dollar-value does the Federal Aviation Administration assign to each statistical life saved when evaluating its policies?
3. According to Hahn, why will the policies fail to have a significant impact on airline terrorism?

Excerpted from Robert W. Hahn, "The Cost of Antiterrorist Rhetoric," *Regulation*, vol. 19, no. 4, 1996. Reprinted by permission of the Cato Institute.

Improving [aviation] security is important, but we need to assess the cost and effectiveness of each measure before spending billions of taxpayers' and travelers' dollars on security-enhancing measures. Moreover, we need to confront the question of how safe is safe enough. The sad truth is that the threat of airline terrorism cannot be eliminated unless air travel is banned, and that is simply too high a price to pay. So some level of risk must be deemed acceptable. This viewpoint provides a framework for thinking about these risk tradeoffs by examining the costs and benefits of policies selected for reducing terrorism.

SAFETY MEASURES AND TRAVEL DELAYS

In the post-TWA crash world [TWA Flight 800 crashed in July 1996], airline travelers can easily tell you about the costs they have incurred. Passengers must arrive at airports earlier, stand in longer lines, answer more questions about the contents of their carryon bags, and show photo identifications before boarding.

Implementing [the White House Commission on Aviation Safety and Security, headed by Vice President Al Gore] proposals will lead to even more lines and delays. A rough calculation of the annual costs of delays can be made by multiplying the number of passengers affected by the additional wait by the value of their time. In 1995, travelers took approximately 390 million trips on U.S. airlines. The Federal Aviation Administration (FAA) and the airlines recommended arriving at the airport thirty minutes earlier than normal because of the security measures implemented in July 1995. The FAA, in its calculations, uses a value-of-time estimate of $48 an hour for business travelers and $42 an hour for nonbusiness travelers in 1995 dollars. This yields an estimate of $9 billion per year in delay costs. Even if the FAA's value of time were halved, the annual cost of a thirty-minute delay would be over $4 billion. As air travel becomes more costly, people will choose alternative forms of transportation, which will likely reduce delay costs about 3 percent. . . .

PROBLEMATIC PROPOSALS

Some of the important and controversial proposals of the Gore Commission have been analyzed by researchers, and their findings do not inspire confidence. Examples of the commission's proposals include the use of explosive detection devices, automated passenger profiling, and passenger-bag matching.

The General Accounting Office (GAO) has reviewed the state of the explosive detection technologies and the FAA's efforts to improve airport security. The GAO found that explosive screening technologies are not particularly reliable; they frequently yield false alarms, and they do not process baggage as quickly as claimed. The FAA has only certified one explosive detection machine (CTX 5000) for checked baggage screening. The certified machine has an actual "throughput rate" that is much less than the designed rate of five hundred bags per hour; thus, two units are necessary to meet the FAA's throughput requirement. Even with two machines, there is significant potential for operator error. It seems likely, for example, that in the press of rush hour, operators will start ignoring "positives" to reduce the ire of busy travelers.

Delays associated with this technology could be quite expensive. If enough machines are not deployed, slow screening of baggage may result in significant delays. False alarms could lead to hundreds or even thousands of bags needing additional inspection. If this technology leads to delays, airlines would have to react by scheduling longer turnaround times that would probably decrease the number of flights and, in turn, increase ticket prices. Moreover, it would cost up to $2.2 billion just to acquire and install these machines in the seventy-five busiest airports in the United States.

AVIATION TERRORISM IS NOT A REAL THREAT

There is not now, and has not been in the past, an epidemic of terrorists sneaking bombs onto airplanes in this country. Heck, we hardly even hear of a hijacking anymore.

It's sad but true: Air travelers are being subjected to all sorts of expensive, inconvenient security measures that do absolutely nothing to make travel safer, because their purpose is to combat a threat that doesn't exist.

Bill Thompson, North County Times, October 5, 1997.

A second proposal, automated passenger profiling, would use a computer database with information on passenger characteristics to determine who could be a terrorist and thus require further scrutiny. This process could reduce the number of bags that must be further scrutinized by up to 80 percent and may be a cost-effective approach to reducing terrorism; but, there are some potential problems with its implementation. The American Civil Liberties Union (ACLU) protests the use of profiling, arguing that it is unreliable and discriminatory. As the ACLU pointed out in testimony before the White House Commission, the actual saboteur does not always fit the profile of a terrorist. There have also been cases where passengers who "fit the profile" have been detained and questioned for hours, although they were not guilty of wrongdoing.

A third proposal is "positive passenger-bag matches," which would ensure that each bag on every flight is accompanied by a passenger. If a passenger fails to board a flight, his checked luggage would be removed. Passenger-bag matching will prevent the "drop and run" terrorist tactic but will not stop those who are tricked into carrying explosives or the determined saboteur who is willing to give up his own life.

BAG MATCHING RAISES CONCERNS

There is particular cause for concern with the proposal to require full passenger-bag matches for all domestic flights. The process of bag matching can be very time consuming. In 1989, then-Transportation Secretary Sam Skinner testified to Congress that this type of requirement for domestic flights "would probably paralyze" the air transport hub system. For example, if a passenger fails to board a plane, it could take several hours to remove his bags from a luggage container on a large plane.

Currently, bag matches are required by the FAA for international flights. International travelers are requested to arrive two hours early to allow time for all the inspections. If this requirement for domestic flights causes about the same delay as for international flights, each passenger could spend an additional hour in the airport. This would increase the expected delay cost from $9 to $18 billion. But considering the larger scale of the domestic market (international passengers account for less than 10 percent of U.S. carriers' passengers), actual delays and delay costs could be much greater.

The positive bag-match requirement and the new explosive detection technology introduce another important delay cost that is not easily quantified—the anxiety of missing a flight because of unpredictable security delays. This cost has not been explicitly considered in any of the proposals endorsed by the Gore Commission, even though it is likely to be significant in some cases.

Although [President Clinton] asked and received from Congress over $400 million to implement the initial proposals, the actual annual cost of implementation would be in the billions. Implementing full passenger-bag match alone will cost $2 billion annually and, as previously noted, the initial cost of deploying explosive detection devices to screen checked baggage is $2.2 billion. Moreover, the initial cost of machines aimed at screening passengers for explosives would be approximately $1.9 billion.

HIGH COSTS AND MEDIOCRE RESULTS

What will these increased expenditures in time and money buy the American public in terms of security? In a "best case scenario" these changes could eliminate or substantially reduce the threat of airline terrorism. Counter-terrorist expert Michael Ledeen maintains that checking identification, tickets, and baggage more carefully is a good idea; but, even with these enhanced procedures, he believes most earlier terrorist incidents still would have occurred.

Given the paucity of information on benefits, we can develop a scenario based on the assumption that the threat from airline terrorism is completely eliminated. Since 1982, 548 people died in U.S. carrier incidents of sabotage, including TWA flight 800, or about thirty-seven people a year. Dividing this number into the cost estimates for current heightened security measures yields an annual cost per life saved of over $200 million. Excluding the TWA crash, this number would jump to a cost per life saved of well over $300 million. To put this number into perspective, a review of studies suggests that the implicit value of life for air travelers falls between $5 and $15 million. The FAA uses a value of $2.3 million per statistical life saved in evaluating its policies.

If historical trends are indicative of future terrorist threats, the number of deaths prevented is likely to substantially overstate the benefits because the measures are not likely to be very effective in deterring terrorists. Nonetheless, I cannot rule out the scenario that terrorist activity could increase dramatically over my baseline estimates. There would need to be a ten- to one-hundredfold increase in the number of lives saved before this investment would be as attractive as alternative methods of saving lives. A number of life-saving investments required by the Department of Transportation, such as side impact standards for automobiles and cabin fire protection in aircraft, have been over two hundred times more cost-effective than these proposals.

Some may argue that even if the security measures are not very effective, people benefit psychologically by believing they will work. I cannot refute this argument directly. It may be that people are willing to pay large sums to feel safer, but I think a strong argument can be made that, absent concrete research supporting this assertion, the money would be far better spent by leaving it in the hands of taxpayers or having the government spend it on safety measures that will save more lives, and at a substantially lower cost. . . .

While we do not know the final outcome of the Gore Commission proposals, they contain some important flaws. First, the policies are likely to have a minimal impact on airline terrorism—precisely because they do not dramatically increase the cost of carrying out terrorist acts. Terrorists will find the weakest link in the chain that will serve their purposes. If some U.S. airports and flights become less vulnerable, they will go after other targets, such as smaller airports.

Second, in some cases, the policies are too centralized. Notwithstanding the potential problems with a rigorous passenger bag-match requirement for domestic flights, airlines and airports would be forced to comply with such a regulation if the FAA requires it. Another example is contained in the provision that shifts responsibility to the National Transportation Safety Board for working directly with the families of air accident victims. As a representative of United Airlines points out, this will merely add another step in the emergency response process. The airlines possess information and resources to assist family members that government agencies would not have.

Third, to the extent possible, the beneficiaries of the antiterrorist measures should be those who foot the bill. Unfortunately, this principle appears to have been ignored in the current legislation. The initial appropriations under the new antiterrorist laws will be paid for by taxpayers. The administration has argued that airline terrorism is a matter of national security, but the primary beneficiaries of the antiterrorist measures would be air travelers. If this is true, then air travelers should be asked to pay the lion's share of the cost.

The government's reaction to the TWA crash is both predictable and problematic. Our elected officials, including the president, have allowed the cart to go before the horse, by passing a piece of legislation based on emotion rather than reason. Fortunately, however, there is one reason to be optimistic: not much damage has been done yet. The recent spate of antiterrorist laws leaves a great deal of flexibility with the FAA in developing regulations. If the regulations are developed judiciously, then some useful policy changes could be introduced. But such policy changes are unlikely to emerge unless we can learn from our regulatory successes and failures.

Terrorism is likely to be with us for the foreseeable future. Moreover, in a more open world, it becomes more difficult to contain. We should zealously attempt to contain it, but we should be wary of giving up our freedom and our time before having a reasonable idea of what we will get in return for these sacrifices.

"Terrorists respect ruthlessness, being ruthless themselves."

THE UNITED STATES SHOULD RETALIATE AGAINST TERRORIST GROUPS

Holger Jensen

In the following viewpoint, Holger Jensen argues that the United States' response to terrorism has been weak and ineffective and that America needs to become more aggressive in its fight against international terrorism. Jensen asserts that the United States should follow the lead of nations such as Russia and Israel and retaliate against terrorists. However, he acknowledges, the United States often faces criticism when it attacks nations such as Iraq and Sudan, partly because many foreign observers question the motivations of the Clinton administration. Jensen is the international editor of the *Rocky Mountain News*.

As you read, consider the following questions:

1. How many hostages did Hezbollah and other terrorist organizations take during the 1980s, according to the author?
2. According to Jensen, why might the military strikes in Sudan and Afghanistan lead to further violence?
3. According to the author, what does being a civilized nation entail?

Reprinted from Holger Jensen, "United States Should Take Cue from Terrorists Themselves," *Rocky Mountain News*, August 25, 1998, by permission of NewsQuest.

In 1983, terrorist car bombs killed nearly 300 Americans at the U.S. Embassy in Beirut and Marine barracks south of the Lebanese capital.

The attacks were quickly pinned on Shiite Muslim fanatics of Hezbollah, the Iranian-backed Party of God. Washington vowed vengeance; U.S. warships made threatening moves in the eastern Mediterranean, but there were no reprisals.

At about the same time, three Soviet diplomats were kidnapped and killed in Beirut. Moscow issued no statements and made no threats. But pretty soon dead Shiites began showing up all over the city. They had been castrated and horribly tortured.

Whether the KGB did the "wet work" or contracted it out to free-lance assassins, of whom there were plenty in Beirut at the time, will never be known. But the message was not lost on Shiite terrorists. Not a single Russian was ever harmed again.

HOLDING AMERICANS HOSTAGE

Americans remained fair game, however.

Over the next few years, Hezbollah and its offshoots, operating under a variety of names, seized 90 foreign hostages, including 17 Americans.

Eleven were killed or died in captivity and 79 were ultimately freed, among them Associated Press correspondent Terry Anderson and Coloradan Thomas Sutherland.

The identity and headquarters of the kidnappers were well-known to U.S. intelligence agencies, as Anderson subsequently found out, but no attempts were made to rescue the hostages or exact reprisals. The last remaining captives were freed only after arduous negotiations by Terry Waite, an emissary from the archbishop of Canterbury who was himself kidnapped for a while, and then U.N. Secretary-General Peres de Cuellar, who persuaded Iran that keeping American hostages had no value after the U.S. victory in the Persian Gulf War.

Anderson blames his own government more than his kidnappers for 6½ lost years.

Washington's inaction may also be blamed for a host of subsequent terrorist attacks on Americans or U.S. interests worldwide, not only by Islamic extremists but other terrorist groups encouraged by the lack of reprisals.

INADEQUATE RETALIATIONS

The Clinton administration did retaliate for Iraq's abortive attempt to assassinate President Bush in Kuwait in 1993. Navy ships lobbed 24 cruise missiles at the headquarters of Baghdad's intelligence agency, but it was in the dead of night when the building was empty of senior officials. The missiles did nothing to intimidate Iraqi President Saddam Hussein.

There were no reprisals for the 1996 bombing of Khobar Towers near Dhahran, Saudi Arabia, that killed 19 U.S. airmen and wounded 500. Significantly, that attack was blamed on Osama bin Laden, the shadowy Saudi millionaire who holes up in Afghanistan, bankrolls a variety of terrorist groups and now is accused of being behind the bombing of U.S. embassies in Nairobi and Dar es Salaam [in August 1998].

Again the Clinton administration chose cruise missiles to retaliate, striking a terrorist training camp in Afghanistan and a pharmaceutical plant in Sudan suspected of manufacturing chemical weapons.

Bin Laden's terrorist network runs training camps in both countries and is suspected of producing chemical arms at a secret facility in Sudan. However, there is some question as to whether the El Shifa Pharmaceutical Industries Company in Khartoum was a front for such activities. It was Sudan's largest producer of antibiotics, malaria medicines and veterinary drugs and had a profitable export business.

Even if it did produce chemical precursors, as National Security Adviser Sandy Berger maintains, many question the wisdom of fighting terrorism with missiles.

FIGHT TERROR WITH TERROR

Terrorists respect ruthlessness, being ruthless themselves. But it must be highly selective, fought in secret, targeting only those responsible and never acknowledging guilt. The Russians demonstrated such ruthlessness in Beirut. The Israelis, too, have perfected the art of fighting terror with terror.

Despite some spectacular foul-ups—such as the killing of a Danish waiter in Copenhagen and the botched assassination of a Hamas operative in Amman, Jordan—Mossad has racked up a deadly record of hits on Palestinian terrorists without ever bragging about it. The terrorists know who did it, and that's enough for the Israelis.

In contrast, the American response to terrorism seems clumsy and ineffective.

Our government imposes sanctions on so-called rogue nations that sponsor terrorism—which hasn't altered their behavior one bit—but makes no effort to go after the terrorists on the ground. In most cases it does not even retaliate for terrorist attacks.

In some cases it tries to make terrorists or countries that sponsor them respect the rule of law, when both operate well outside it. A classic case is Libya. A decade after Libyan terrorists blew up Pan Am Flight 103 over Lockerbie, Scotland, the United States is still trying to persuade Libya to surrender the suspects and is dickering about where they should be tried.

SOME RETALIATION IS CRITICIZED

In the few instances where there has been retaliation, such as President Reagan's bombing of Libya and President Clinton's use of Tomahawk missiles, the military overkill and "ancillary damage"—a polite euphemism for civilian casualties—cause international outrage that wipes out whatever sympathy was generated for the victims of the terrorist attack that prompted the reprisal.

Reprinted by permission of Chuck Asay and Creators Syndicate.

The embassy bombings in Kenya and Tanzania had been universally condemned, not least because the blasts aimed at Americans also killed or maimed thousands of innocent Africans. But Clinton's missile strikes on Afghanistan and Sudan immediately redirected that anger toward the United States, which was accused of practicing its own brand of terrorism against those two well-known state sponsors of terrorism.

In terms of deterrence, the Tomahawks achieved nothing. In fact, they may provoke even more terrorism. Bin Laden is uncowed and, according to a newspaper in Karachi, Pakistan, offering a $100,000 reward for every American killed. Some Islamic nations that initially condemned him have now joined in his calls for revenge.

There would, of course, be a similar outcry if U.S. Special Forces troops raided bin Laden's headquarters in Afghanistan and actually succeeded in killing him. But such a mission would be secretly admired, even by its critics, and it would send a message to other terrorist masterminds that the United States will go to any lengths to put them out of business.

Of course, that will never happen. Being a civilized nation, we have officially renounced the use of assassination and other extralegal means to fight terrorism. And poll-driven presidents don't dare send American troops into harm's way, especially in an election year, when they can score more points by simply lobbing missiles from the safety of American ships at sea.

CLINTON'S MOTIVES ARE QUESTIONABLE

It may not hurt him at home but it does not help us abroad that Clinton had just confessed to a sexual dalliance with a White House intern. Even some of our allies questioned Clinton's motive in ordering a missile strike only two days after his mea culpa.

His previous missile attacks on Iraq—variously blamed on Whitewater, Gennifer Flowers and Paula Jones—have reinforced a widely held foreign perception that Clinton likes to throw Tomahawks around whenever he wants to distract Americans from his domestic travails.

It can be, of course, argued that the president's sex life is nobody's business but his own, with no bearing on how he conducts himself in the face of terrorism. But it does affect his conduct of U.S. foreign policy and our nation's influence abroad.

When rioting mobs in Pakistan hold up signs blaming Monica Lewinsky for Clinton's missile flexing, the president's "lapse of judgment" becomes our business.

"Launching unmanned missiles at
distant targets as ill-defined as 'the
infrastructure of terrorism' is . . .
[not] a credible deterrent against
future criminal acts."

RETALIATION EFFORTS AGAINST
TERRORISTS ARE FRUITLESS

Raymond Close

On August 20, 1998, the United States ordered military strikes
in Sudan and Afghanistan in response to the bombings of American embassies in Kenya and Tanzania earlier that month. In the
following viewpoint, Raymond Close asserts that such a response does not reduce terrorism and weakens the United
States' diplomatic standing in the world. He contends that the
United States should not follow the lead of nations that answer
terrorism with violence, such as Israel, because those nations
have failed to solve the problem. In addition, Close claims the
attacks in Sudan and Afghanistan may inflame militant Islam organizations and lead to future terrorist bombings. Close served
in the Central Intelligence Agency for 26 years.

As you read, consider the following questions:

1. In Close's view, what is terrorism's best asset?
2. Why will terrorism persist in Israel, according to the author?
3. According to Close, what is the worst nightmare of America's
   military planners?

Reprinted from Raymond Close, "How Not to Fight Terrorism," *The Washington Post National
Weekly Edition*, September 7, 1998, by permission of the author.

My first job for the CIA's clandestine services 46 years ago was to organize a network of informants in the squalid Palestinian refugee camps of southern Lebanon—some, ironically, barely a stone's throw from where my grandfather and great-grandfather established American mission schools more than a hundred years ago. The camps and the squalor are still there, no longer breeding grounds of communism as they were in the 1950s, but of the threat called terrorism.

Most of us accept the premise that terrorism is a phenomenon that can be defeated only by better ideas, by persuasion and, most importantly, by amelioration of the conditions that inspire it. Terrorism's best asset, in the final analysis, is the fire in the bellies of its young men, and that fire cannot be extinguished by Tomahawk missiles. If intelligent Americans can accept that premise as a reasonable basis for dealing with this nemesis, why is it so difficult for our leaders to speak and act accordingly?

A DANGEROUS PRECEDENT

After the military strikes in Sudan and Afghanistan [on August 20, 1998, in response to the bombings of the U.S. embassies in Kenya and Tanzania], U.S. officials justified their action by citing Osama bin Laden's "declaration of war" on everything American. But to launch missiles into countries with which we are technically at peace—and to kill their citizens—is to declare that the United States is free to make its own rules for dealing with this international problem. What standing will we have in the future to complain about any other country that attacks the territory of its neighbor, citing as justification the need to protect itself from terrorism? Did those who authorized these attacks think through the long-term implications of this short-sighted and dangerous precedent?

Let's get down to practical realities. The new threat we face is often stateless, without sovereign territory or official sponsorship. Friendly governments around the world—especially those with large Muslim populations such as India, Pakistan, Egypt, Turkey, Jordan, Indonesia, Malaysia, the Gulf states and the new republics of Central Asia—share a common need for internal and regional stability. Terrorism is a weapon that threatens all civil authority. This set of circumstances provides an unprecedented incentive for intergovernmental cooperation, even among states that may differ on other basic issues. But the fight against a silent and hidden common enemy requires infinite patience and tact on the part of law enforcement agencies and intelligence services. It demands absolute secrecy, mutual trust and professional respect. If the United States loses its cool without warning, if it is seen by others as a loose cannon that resorts to sudden violent action on a massive scale, the critically needed cooperation will not be there.

My hunch is that the next time we call for help (from Pakistan, for instance, whose very competent police work was evidently vital to the investigation of the Nairobi and Dar es Salaam bombings), the officials of that country's intelligence service who are responsible for discreet liaison with the CIA or the FBI will be conveniently "out to lunch." My ex-colleagues at the Agency, and the experienced professionals at the Bureau, must be worried about this. They live on shared confidence. They know how hard it is to develop trust, and how quickly it can evaporate.

Do Not Follow Israel's Lead

In declaring a full-scale war on terrorism, the Clinton administration seems tempted to emulate Israel's failed example. This is understandable, but wrong. Israel's situation is totally different from ours in every imaginable way. The state of Israel has been committed for 50 years to a policy of massive and ruthless retaliation—deliberately disproportional. "Ten eyes for an eye," the Israelis like to say. And still their policy fails, because they have not recognized what the thoughtful ones among them know to be true—that terrorism will thrive as long as the Palestinian population is obsessed with the injustice of their lot and consumed with despair. Wise and experienced Israeli intelligence officials have conceded to me that the brilliantly "successful" assassination of a Palestinian terrorist leader in Gaza a couple of years ago led directly to the series of suicide bombings that helped bring Israeli Prime Minister Binyamin Netanyahu to power—and may thereby have set back Israel's chances for peace for many years to come.

Even those who approve in theory of using military retaliation as a weapon against terrorism would agree, I think, that launching unmanned missiles at distant targets as ill-defined as "the infrastructure of terrorism" is neither an effective military strategy nor a credible deterrent against future criminal acts. This will be even more true when the adversary is armed some day with cheap, do-it-yourself weapons of mass destruction. In our understandable frustration, are we resorting to a modern form of the same "gunboat diplomacy" that proved so counterproductive for the dying European empires at the end of the 19th century?

Over several years, the United States has tried vainly to control Iraq's behavior by launching similar kinds of stand-off strikes against Saddam Hussein. Throwing rocks at him from a safe distance at least had the merit of making us feel good, and we justified it by protesting that "we had to do *something!*" Our policymakers have concluded that this wasn't working. It was costing us a small fortune, severely weakening the overall combat readiness of our armed forces, straining relations with our allies, abetting the interests of our antagonists and economic competitors, and probably only strengthening the grip that Hussein holds on his suffering people.

© Andy Singer. Reprinted with permission.

So when Hussein again defied the U.N. inspection regime in 1998, we mumbled some weak excuses and pretended we hadn't noticed. Now, by launching attacks against suspected terrorist targets in Afghanistan and Sudan and threatening more violent retaliation in the event of further incidents, we have started down that same dead-end road—committing ourselves to actions that we may be unable or unwilling to take under unpredictable future circumstances. This move, seemingly inspired more by exasperation than cool reason, violates basic rules of both diplomacy and warfare.

DEMONIZATION IS DANGEROUS

President Clinton and others have labeled all Islamic terrorists as members or "affiliates" of the "Osama bin Laden Network of Terrorism." This is, of course, the common mistake of demonizing one individual as the root of all evil. In fact, elevating bin Laden to that status only gives him a mantle of heroism now and, more ominously, will guarantee him martyrdom if he should die.

Informed students of the subject have known for years that although the various militant Islamist movements around the world share a common ideology and many of the same grievances, they are not a monolithic international organization. Our attacks, unfortunately, may have inflamed their common zeal and hastened their unification and centralization—while probably adding hosts of new volunteers to their ranks. We are rolling up a big snowball.

The worst nightmare of our strategic military and security planners is that a small and weak enemy could hold us hostage by possessing a weapon of monstrous power, yet so insignificant in size and appearance that we cannot see it, cannot locate it, and therefore cannot attack and destroy it. The recent military strikes sent the message again, loudly and clearly, to all who would count themselves as our enemies: Accelerate your efforts to acquire new and deadly high-technology weapons—and manufacture and store those weapons in hard shelters in the midst of your civilian population. American policymakers and military planners have an obligation to evaluate every proposed action by the standard of whether it will help postpone the day when this nightmare may come true. I believe our leadership failed to do so before [August 1998's] operations.

AMERICA SHOULD BE JUST AND FAIR

Meanwhile, the bombing, portrayed as necessary to forestall additional terrorist acts, has produced a level of public alarm in Washington that is precisely what the terrorists hoped to inspire. We forget, of course, that if the terrorist has any outstanding quality besides vengefulness and cunning, it is patience. He may strike back next week, next month or next year. The ludicrous image of four-star American generals emptying their pockets of coins and keys before passing through the metal detectors at the Pentagon seems to me starkly symbolic of the futility of retaliatory violence. What have we done to ourselves?

What worries me most, in the final analysis, is that our attacks on the targets in Afghanistan and Sudan were reminiscent of what we call "vigilante justice" in American folklore. This kind of policy weakens our leadership position in the world and undermines the most effective defenses we will have against the terrorist threat: a commitment to the rule of law, dedication to fairness and evenhandedness in settling international disputes and a reputation as the most humanitarian nation in the world.

"Law enforcement agencies can and must do everything within their power to prevent terrorist incidents from occurring."

EXPANDING THE FBI'S POWERS IS A NECESSARY RESPONSE TO TERRORISM

Louis J. Freeh

In the following viewpoint, Federal Bureau of Investigation (FBI) director Louis J. Freeh argues that the FBI needs expanded powers in order to respond to terrorism effectively. According to Freeh, additional resources and personnel will enable the FBI to investigate groups and individuals that advocate the use of deadly violence. In addition, Freeh asserts, the FBI can use its skills to respond to terrorist acts after they occur and help apprehend those who committed the crimes. This viewpoint was written prior to the April 1996 passage of the "Antiterrorism and Effective Death Penalty Act of 1996," which included $1 billion to help federal and state authorities fight terrorism.

As you read, consider the following questions:

1. What was one of the Unabomber's stated goals, as cited by Freeh?
2. When did the FBI begin its involvement in counterterrorism, according to the author?
3. According to Freeh, why do law enforcement agencies need wireless communication devices?

Reprinted from Louis J. Freeh, "What Can Be Done About Terrorism?" USA Today magazine, January 1996, by permission of the Society for the Advancement of Education; ©1996.

The bombing of the Murrah Federal Building in Oklahoma City brought terrorism to the nation's heartland. It also brought terrorism into countless living rooms across the nation—with images so graphic they shall not, indeed can not, be forgotten. This was another example of the immense suffering Americans have endured at the hands of terrorists:

A CHRONOLOGY OF TERRORISM

• April 1983: The U.S. Embassy in Beirut, Lebanon, was bombed, leaving 16 dead and more than 100 injured.

• October 1983: The U.S. Marine barracks in Beirut was bombed, resulting in 241 deaths.

• June 1985: TWA Flight 847 was hijacked. U.S. Navy diver Robert Stethem, who was on board, was brutally murdered, his body dumped on the airport tarmac.

• February 1988: Marine Lt. Col. William Higgins—part of the United Nations peacekeeping force in Lebanon—was kidnapped and later murdered.

• December 1988: Pan Am Flight 103 was blown up over Lockerbie, Scotland, with 270 killed.

• February 1993: New York City's World Trade Center was bombed by Islamic extremists, leaving six dead and hundreds injured.

• March 1995: American diplomatic personnel were murdered in a hail of machine gun fire on the streets of Karachi, Pakistan.

Terrorists also perpetrated the murder of athletes at the 1972 Munich Summer Olympics, bombings in Buenos Aires, Paris, and London, and poison gas attacks in Tokyo's subway system.

Although there are different types of terrorism, one common thread in all of these dreadful crimes is that the innocent suffer. Too many Americans have been victimized by terrorists, in the U.S. and other countries.

HATRED CAUSES TERRORISM

It is essential that terrorism be viewed in broad terms. Inevitably, it is fueled by extreme hatred. Those who harbor such hatred live in a world that is colored by bigotry, shaded by conspiracy, and framed by ignorance. Some claim there are plots to take control of the world's financial markets and the mass media and to surrender the U.S. to foreign military control. Others direct their ire at corporate America and evolving technology. Paranoia drives some to lash out at anyone unlike themselves.

Take the Unabomber suspect, for example. This self-described terrorist, who is responsible for murdering three persons and injuring 23 others, followed up a 1995 mail bomb with a letter to *The New York Times*. In it, he said that he killed a business executive in December 1994, because Thomas Mosser worked for a company whose "business is the development of techniques for manipulating people's attitudes." In that same letter, the bomber wrote: "The people we are out to get are the scientists and engineers, especially in critical fields like computers and genetics." Among the Unabomber's stated goals is "the destruction of the worldwide industrial system." Lengthy excerpts of his manifesto were published in the *Washington Post* and *The New York Times* on Aug. 1, 1995, followed by a 35,000-word manuscript in the *Post* on Sept. 19, when he promised to cease the bombings if they printed both. [In 1998, Theodore Kaczynski admitted he was the Unabomber. He was sentenced to life in prison.] . . .

Bold steps are needed to combat terrorists—and the Federal Bureau of Investigation (FBI) is taking them. For instance, we committed every necessary resource in order to resolve fully the deadly bombing in Oklahoma City, just as we did in New York City, when the World Trade Center was bombed in February 1993. I have strengthened the FBI's Counterterrorism Program by re-assigning hundreds of special agents to investigate these offenses. However, we need more investigative tools to improve the ability of the U.S. to respond to the terrorist threat. At the same time, I recognize that these tools must be used carefully and must preserve the individual liberties and constitutional rights that are so essential in our democracy.

INVESTIGATIONS ARE NEEDED

In this regard, I applaud the leadership that President Clinton and Attorney General Janet Reno have shown. They understand that—consistent with America's democratic traditions—more must be done to fight terrorists. Thus, the President has proposed specific steps to be taken—including resource and personnel enhancements. Just as in a time of war, both political parties have agreed to put aside partisan differences while considering those measures.

The FBI is not seeking broad and undefined intelligence collection abilities. Nevertheless, law enforcement agencies have to know as much as possible about those individuals and groups that are advocating deadly violence in furtherance of their causes.

I do not urge investigative activity against persons or groups exercising their legitimate constitutional rights. Nor do I suggest that we should target people who simply disagree with our government. We all are bound by the Constitution, due process considerations, and the American legal system. Each of them protects the American people and those who serve in law enforcement.

The FBI is not looking to investigate lawful activity. It is not concerned about people or groups because of their ideology or philosophy. As I testified before Congress in April 1995, "We do not need the business. The FBI has lots of important work to do in protecting the people and the United States."

A COMPLICATED MISSION

The FBI's involvement in counterterrorism is not something new. It dates back to 1982, when President Ronald Reagan designated the FBI as the lead agency for countering terrorism in the U.S. Those responsibilities further were expanded in 1984 and 1986, when Congress passed laws giving the FBI authority to investigate crimes of terrorism abroad against Americans, such as murder and hostage-taking.

The FBI's counterterrorism mission is fairly simple to state, but perhaps not so easy to carry out. It is to prevent acts of terrorism *before* they occur and/or react to them *after* they occur by bringing the perpetrators to justice.

Court-authorized wiretaps are one means that law enforcement agencies use to prevent crimes from occurring. In this connection, encryption capabilities available to terrorists and other criminals endanger the future usefulness of court-authorized wiretaps. If law enforcement is to do its job effectively, this issue must be resolved.

Law enforcement agencies have another acute technological need. They must have the ability to communicate rapidly by radio and other forms of wireless communications. Local, state, and Federal law enforcement officers and agencies must be able to talk among themselves, so that a state trooper patrolling America's highways in any state has the full benefit of law enforcement's knowledge when he approaches a car with a suspect in it.

Prevention means that, through investigation, we get there before the bomb goes off, before the plane is hijacked, before innocent Americans lose their lives. This is our number-one priority.

RESPONSES TO TERRORIST ATTACKS

Reaction is the law enforcement response after the fact. Although it has been over seven years since the bombing of Pan Am Flight 103, the perpetrators still have not been brought to justice. The U.S. government has not forgotten the case, though. On November 14, 1991, the Department of Justice obtained indictments against the two Libyan intelligence operatives allegedly responsible for the bombing—Lamen Khalifa Fhimah and Abdel Basset Ali Al-Megrahi.

Since the bombing, the UN has issued several resolutions in an attempt to force Libya to end its sponsorship of terrorism, accept responsibility for the Pan Am 103 bombing, and extradite Fhimah and Megrahi to either the U.S. or the United Kingdom to stand trial.

SOME RIGHTS SHOULD BE REVISED

Advocates of absolute civil liberties forget that legally protected freedoms are not *ends* in and of themselves; they are *means* to ensuring the health and well-being of the citizens. The United States Constitution, said Justice Robert Jackson, is not a suicide pact. And when a protected "right" in practice results in the encouragement and breeding of terrorist monstrosities ready to devour other members of society, then it is clear that such a right has ceased to serve its true end and must be either revised or reduced.

Benjamin Netanyahu, *Fighting Terrorism: How Democracies Can Defeat Domestic and International Terrorists*, 1995.

In March 1995, Fhimah and Megrahi were added to the FBI's Ten Most Wanted Fugitives List. The same day, the State Department allocated up to $4,000,000 of reward money for information leading to their arrest.

There is a need for adoption of tougher worldwide antiterrorism measures. The FBI works closely with many of its counterparts around the globe. We have found them eager to join in this common battle.

As of 1996, the FBI has 23 legal attaches overseas—FBI agents working hand in hand with law enforcement officials from the host nations to address the growing, joint problems of terrorism and other international crimes. These agents are the U.S.'s first line of law enforcement defense overseas. To combat the many and varying forms of terrorism, the FBI needs more legal attaches in other nations around the world to investigate jointly and control these types of criminal acts.

THE FBI AND OVERSEAS INVESTIGATIONS

All of the FBI's overseas counterterrorism investigations are conducted in close coordination with the U.S. Department of State and with the approval and support of the foreign countries where the terrorist incidents occur or may develop. For example, when

Pan Am Flight 103 exploded over Lockerbie, Scotland, the FBI didn't just take over the criminal investigation. We were *asked* by the British and Scottish authorities to participate, and our activities abroad closely were coordinated with the State Department.

In April 1995, under the FBI's leadership, the International Law Enforcement Academy opened in Budapest, Hungary. There, law enforcement officials from 22 nations throughout Central and Eastern Europe and the countries of the former Soviet Union will receive training in a wide variety of matters. Through the Academy, law enforcement around the world will expand its network, thereby enhancing the ability to combat—consistent with the rule of law—those who would engage in terrorism.

Law enforcement agencies can and must do everything within their power to prevent terrorist incidents from occurring. Where prevention programs fail, as they sometimes do, we must do our very best to apprehend and convict the terrorists—to see that justice is served. We owe it to the memories of their victims.

"The 'Public Safety Act' is the
nastiest piece of legislation that
[Bill] Clinton has signed during his
first term."

COUNTERTERRORISM LEGISLATION
IS A DANGEROUS EXPANSION OF
GOVERNMENTAL POWERS

Jeffrey Rosen

The "Effective Death Penalty and Public Safety Act of 1996"
[also known as the "Antiterrorism and Effective Death Penalty
Act of 1996"] poses a threat to civil liberties, argues Jeffrey
Rosen in the following viewpoint. He asserts that the bill endan-
gers civil liberties by weakening habeas corpus laws and including provisions that make it easier for the government to deport
immigrants. In addition, Rosen maintains that the bill will have
little impact on fighting terrorism. Rosen is the legal affairs editor for the *New Republic* and an associate professor of law at
George Washington University in Washington, D.C.

As you read, consider the following questions:

1. According to Rosen, what alliance did the Justice Department
   blame for the terrorism bill?
2. Why will the changes in habeas corpus fail to have an impact
   on the fight against terrorism, in the author's view?
3. What does Rosen find ironic about the terrorism bill?

Reprinted from Jeffrey Rosen, "Shell Game," *The New Republic*, May 13, 1996, by
permission of *The New Republic*. Copyright ©1996 by The New Republic, Inc.

"I weep for you," the Walrus said:
  "I deeply sympathize."
With sobs and tears he sorted out
  Those of the largest size
Holding his pocket-handkerchief
  Before his streaming eyes.

"**H**e's very upset," says a senior administration official of President Clinton's decision to sign the "Effective Death Penalty and Public Safety Act of 1996." "It breaks his heart." On the one hand, Clinton was reluctant to go down in history as the president who signed the first statutory limitations on habeas corpus since Magna Carta; on the other hand, there was Oklahoma City. So, like Lewis Carroll's Walrus, who snuffled over the fate of the oysters even as he devoured every one, Clinton weepily girded himself for the signing ceremony. But never mind the tears. The "Public Safety Act" is the nastiest piece of legislation that Clinton has signed during his first term, and his failure to veto it will be a permanent stain on his presidency.

IDENTIFYING THE VILLAINS

To assuage their jittery consciences, Justice Department officials are suggesting that the real villain in the drama that led to the terrorism bill was the unlikely alliance between the American Civil Liberties Union (ACLU) and the National Rifle Association (NRA). Before Oklahoma City, the administration proposed a series of measures for expanding the Federal Bureau of Investigation's (FBI) power to fight international terrorism, including a good-faith exception for illegally conducted wiretaps and greater access to credit records. Waving the banner of Ruby Ridge, a coalition of liberal civil libertarians and conservative anti-federalists persuaded Representative Bob Barr of Georgia to sponsor an amendment removing the Clinton proposals. As soon as the amendment passed in March 1995, the NRA withdrew its opposition to the terrorism bill, which sailed through the House and Senate with hardly any debate last week. "To me, the lesson is that an alliance between the radical right and the radical left serves the radical right," suggests a senior Justice Department official.

This narrative, however, omits two crucial protagonists: President Clinton and Senator Orrin Hatch. After the Oklahoma City bombing, Hatch saw a heaven-sent opportunity to enact the habeas corpus revolution that Republicans have been proposing for more than a decade. In an inspired bit of ambulance chasing, Hatch dragooned the parents of the Oklahoma bombing victims into endorsing his bill, even though none of them seemed to have a clue what "habeas corpus" meant. (One father confessed he thought it was a high-tech weapon for fighting terrorists.) Clinton, for his part, originally insisted in the wake of the bombing that habeas corpus reform had nothing to do with fighting terrorism. But in June 1995, in one of the most egregious flip flops of his presidency, he announced on "Larry King Live" that habeas corpus reform "ought to be done in the context of this terrorism legislation." Two days later, the Senate obliged.

HABEAS CORPUS HAS BEEN WEAKENED

How radically will the "Public Safety Act" of 1996 change the law of habeas corpus as we know it? Senator Daniel Patrick Moynihan was perhaps a little rash when he compared Clinton's capitulation on habeas corpus to Lincoln's suspension of the Great Writ during the Civil War. Even after the habeas corpus act of 1867, habeas corpus was a relatively thin guarantee that someone couldn't be incarcerated without a judicial hearing in a court of competent jurisdiction. After the Supreme Court's Brown v. Allen decision in 1953, however, habeas corpus was transformed into a mechanism by which federal courts can review the substantive and procedural merits of every conviction (or death penalty) handed down by state courts. The "Effective Death Penalty Act" will essentially return the law to its pre-1953 condition, requiring federal courts to defer to the legal and factual conclusions of state courts, unless the state court determination involved an "unreasonable application of clearly established federal law" or was based on an "unreasonable application of the facts."

This will have no impact at all on fighting terrorists (all of whom are prosecuted in federal rather than state courts in the first place) but will greatly increase the possibility that ordinary defendants can be convicted or executed after a state trial that has been tainted with constitutional or factual errors. Nevertheless, the Rehnquist Court, on its own initiative, has been chipping away at habeas corpus over the past decade; and the Clinton-Hatch bill represents more of a coup de grace for the Warren Court's conception of habeas corpus than a drastic departure from the status quo.

Another land mine buried in the "Public Safety Act" will transform federal-state relations almost as radically as the habeas corpus reforms. Section 702 of the bill federalizes thousands of "assaults with a dangerous weapon" previously punished exclusively under state law, with sentences of up to thirty-five years in a federal prison. At the eleventh hour, on April 15, 1996, the conference committee deleted a requirement that the conduct had to be politically motivated. As the law stands, therefore, the only limitation on what may be the most dramatic federalization of state criminal law in American history is a requirement of criminal "involvement transcending national boundaries." But this could be satisfied by nothing more than evidence that the defendant used drugs imported from Mexico.

AN ILLIBERAL BILL

Finally, there are the immigration provisions. Previously rejected by bipartisan consensus, and smuggled in at the last minute by the conference committee, these provisions would allow the government to deport aliens based on secret evidence; would require the government summarily to exclude aliens who have entered the United States without inspection; and would allow the government to exclude aliens merely on the basis of their membership in illicit organizations. Even the current Supreme Court may well strike down these textbook violations of due process and the First Amendment.

A DRACONIAN LAW

It seems hard to believe that the Republican Congress, so committed to returning powers to the states, and a Democratic president could have concocted such a draconian law—one that enormously increases the power of central government, inserting it further and more insidiously into the daily lives of its citizens. What is more extraordinary is that it passed at a time when there is a heightened sensitivity in both political parties to the outlandish behavior of the federal police, be it the embarrassing scandals surrounding the Central Intelligence Agency (CIA), or the trigger-happy activities of both the Federal Bureau of Investigation (FBI) and the Bureau of Alcohol, Tobacco, and Firearms (BATF).

James Ridgeway, *Village Voice*, May 21, 1996.

It's an irony, and not a very amusing one, that a Congress that pretends to be concerned about states' rights and a president who claims to be devoted to civil liberties have together passed the most illiberal and statist crime bill since the McCarthy era. It will radically expand federal criminal jurisdiction while radically restricting federal courts' ability to review violations of federal constitutional rights. "If you're going to gut the courts and gut the Bill of Rights, you just have a naked federal government that will fulfill the worst nightmares of people who claim they don't want the federal government running everything," says Senator Russell Feingold of Wisconsin, one of only eight senators who found the courage to vote against the bill.

Who deserves more of the blame for this disgraceful law, Clinton or Hatch? "I like the Walrus best," said Alice, "because you see he was a little sorry for the poor oysters." "He ate more than the Carpenter, though," said Tweedledee. "Well," said Alice, "they were both very unpleasant characters."

Periodical Bibliography

The following articles have been selected to supplement the diverse views presented in this chapter. Addresses are provided for periodicals not indexed in the *Readers' Guide to Periodical Literature*, the *Alternative Press Index*, the *Social Sciences Index*, or the *Index to Legal Periodicals and Books*.

Bill Clinton	"The Fight Against Terrorism," *Vital Speeches of the Day*, September 15, 1998.
David Cole	"Terrorizing the Constitution," *Nation*, March 25, 1996.
Mary H. Copper	"Combating Terrorism," *CQ Researcher*, July 21, 1995. Available from 1414 22nd St. NW, Washington, DC 20037.
John Deutch	"Fighting Foreign Terrorism," *Vital Speeches of the Day*, October 1, 1996.
Mark Fischetti	"Defusing Airline Terrorism," *Technology Review*, April 1997.
Philip Heymann	"Listening In on Terrorism," *New York Times*, August 2, 1996.
In These Times	"The Administration Bombs, Again," October 4, 1998.
Vinod K. Jain	"Thwarting Terrorism with Technology," *World & I*, November 1996. Available from 3600 New York Ave. NE, Washington, DC 20002.
Zalmay Khalizad	"Six Steps Against Terror," *Weekly Standard*, August 5, 1996. Available from PO Box 96153, Washington, DC 20090-6153.
Eugene H. Methvin	"Anti-Terrorism: How Far?" *National Review*, July 10, 1995.
New Republic	"Get Personal," September 14–21, 1998.
Daniel Pearl	"Blasting Flap," *Wall Street Journal*, October 28, 1998.
Philip Shenon	"Hitting Home: America Embarks on a New Style of Global War," *New York Times*, August 23, 1998.
Chi Chi Sileo	"The High Price of Antiterrorism," *Insight*, December 18, 1995. Available from 3600 New York Ave. NE, Washington, DC 20002.
David Tucker	"Responding to Terrorism," *Washington Quarterly*, Winter 1998.
Mortimer B. Zuckerman	"It's Time to Fight Back," *U.S. News & World Report*, September 7, 1998.

TERRORISM: A LOOK AT THREE KEY AREAS

MIDDLE EAST

Terrorism in the Middle East has several motivations. One is hatred of the United States, especially its foreign policy. Another motivation is the resentment some Arabs have over the establishment of Israel and their belief that Israel does not have the right to exist. Antagonism to the peace process between Israel and the Palestinian territories also leads to Middle East terrorism.

Terrorism against the United States has included such incidents as the bombing of marine barracks in Beirut, Lebanon, in 1983, the bombing of the Khobar Towers (another military building) in Saudi Arabia in 1996, and the bombing of American embassies in Kenya and Tanzania in 1998. The Lebanese organization Hezbollah was responsible for the Beirut bombing, while Saudi Arabian millionaire Osama Bin Ladin is believed to be the mastermind behind the Khobar and embassy bombings.

Terrorism against Israel has occurred since the nation's inception in 1948. Two major Palestinian organizations that have been linked with terrorism are the Palestine Liberation Organization (PLO) and Hamas. Hezbollah has also been responsible for such terrorism. The PLO was founded in 1964. The Fatah faction of the PLO has allegedly sponsored or launched attacks against Israel. Two of the most well known incidents occurred outside Israel. The first event was the 1972 attack on the Israeli Olympic team in Munich, Germany, in which eleven Israeli athletes and coaches were killed. The second was the 1985 hijacking of the cruise ship *Achille Lauro*, when PLO terrorists shot and killed an elderly Jewish wheelchair-bound passenger and threw him overboard. Hamas, a Palestinian Islamist political group established in 1988, supports a holy war against Israel in order to achieve Palestinian liberation. Its members were closely involved in the Palestinian uprising known as *intifada*, which included such actions as throwing stones and firebombs. However, the *intifada* was generally not viewed as terrorism. Hezbollah has carried out hundreds of attacks against Israeli targets as part of its goal to destroy Israel and liberate Jerusalem.

Since 1979, when the Camp David accords were signed between Israel and Egypt, Israel has sought peace with some of its Arab neighbors, including the Palestinian territories. However, opposition to the Israeli-Palestinian peace process has led to terrorism. While the PLO turned away from terrorism as it gained legitimacy through the peace talks, Hamas has been responsible for numerous suicide bombings, especially on buses or in crowded Israeli marketplaces. Some right-wing extremist Israeli groups also oppose the peace process. The two main organizations are Kach and its offshoot Kahane Chai; these groups' official goal is to restore the biblical state of Israel. Kahane Chai has claimed responsibility for several shooting attacks on Palestinians living in the West Bank region. Individuals responsible for right-wing Israeli terrorism include Baruch Goldstein, who was affiliated with Kach and massacred forty Palestinian worshipers at a mosque in 1994, and Yigal Amir, who assassinated Israeli prime minister Yitzhak Rabin in November 1995.

NORTHERN IRELAND

In 1920, the United Kingdom divided Ireland into two parts, with the larger section becoming the Republic of Ireland and a six-county portion in the northeast (also known as Ulster) remaining part of Britain. Terrorism in Northern Ireland has centered over the dispute as to whether Northern Ireland should be joined with the republic or stay within the United Kingdom.

The Catholic minority in Northern Ireland largely supports joining the Catholic-majority republic, while Ulster's Protestant majority favors retaining the status quo. The major organization favoring a united Ireland is the Irish Republican Army (IRA), established in 1916. Terrorism in Northern Ireland became a problem starting in 1969. During that year, the Provisional IRA split from the Official IRA (which is Marxist-oriented and disavows terrorist actions). The Provisional IRA is synonymous with the IRA and has been responsible for a series of terrorist attacks, notably bombings, assassinations, kidnappings and extortions in Northern Ireland, as well as London. Two notable incidents were the 1979 assassination of Lord Mountbatten, the great-grandson of Queen Victoria and a former viceroy of India, and the 1990 bombing of the London International Stock Exchange. Other groups associated with pro-republic terrorism are the Sinn Fein—the political arm of the IRA—and splinter groups such as the Real IRA and the Continuity IRA.

Those who support Northern Ireland remaining within the United Kingdom have also committed terrorism in the name of their cause. The Royal Ulster Constabulary (RUC) was established in 1922 to serve as the law enforcement organization in Northern Ireland and protect the region from terrorist activities. However, nationalists have accused the RUC and British forces of killing hundreds of civilians. Other groups reportedly responsible for hundreds of deaths are loyalist militias, including the

Loyalist Volunteer Force and the Ulster Volunteer Force. One notorious act of violence against nationalists was the 1972 Bloody Sunday massacre, when British soldiers killed thirteen civilian demonstrators in Derry, Northern Ireland. The massacre led to an increase in IRA terrorist activity.

During the 1990s, the Provisional IRA has started, rescinded, and restarted several cease-fires, while peace talks have progressed between Northern Ireland and the Republic of Ireland. The key players in the peace talks have been Gerry Adams, head of Sinn Fein, David Trimble, leader of the Ulster Unionist Party (which supports remaining part of Britain) and John Hume, the leader of the Social Democratic and Labor Party, Northern Ireland's main Catholic/nationalist party. As of this writing, the Provisional IRA is in a cease-fire but terrorism remains a problem in Ireland, despite the April 1998 peace agreement. In August 1998, a bombing in Omagh, Northern Ireland, left twenty-nine people dead. The Real IRA claimed responsibility for that attack.

UNITED STATES

Terrorism in the United States is both international and domestic. Terrorism by foreign groups and individuals is often motivated by a hatred of the United States, especially U.S. foreign policy in the Middle East. A major incident was the 1993 bombing of the World Trade Center in New York City, which caused six fatalities. That bombing was perpetrated by Middle Eastern terrorists, led by Ramzi Yousef. Yousef and five other suspects have been convicted and sentenced for the crimes. As of this writing, one suspect remains at large.

The United States has also suffered attacks by its own citizens. Hatred of the government—especially taxes and gun control laws—is a common motivation for domestic terrorism. In April 1995, the Alfred P. Murrah federal building in Oklahoma City was bombed, resulting in 169 deaths—the deadliest terrorist attack ever committed on American soil. Timothy McVeigh and Terry Nichols were convicted in the bombing. Both men had ties to militia organizations. While most of these groups, and their members, are law-abiding and pose no threat to the government, others are considered by the Federal Bureau of Investigation (FBI) to be dangerous. McVeigh and Nichols were believed to be motivated in part by anger at what they saw as ruthless behavior by law enforcement. Two seminal events in the early 1990s fomented the tensions between some militia members and the government. One was the August 1992 confrontation between white separatist Randy Weaver and FBI agents, which led to the deaths of Weaver's wife and son and an agent. The other was the 1993 standoff in Waco, Texas, at the Branch Davidian compound, which ended in a deadly fire. Eighty-six compound inhabitants died, including leader David Koresh, though it was unclear how many died from the fire and how many had shot themselves or their cohorts.

Other ideologies motivate terrorism by U.S. citizens. The Unabomber (Theodore Kaczynski) killed three people and injured twenty-three others in mail-bomb attacks between 1978 and 1995. His motivation was not a hatred of government but a hatred of technology. Kaczynski pled guilty in 1998 and was sentenced to life in prison. Pro-life beliefs and radical environmentalism have also motivated other terrorist incidents in the United States.

For Further Discussion

Chapter 1

1. The authors in this chapter offer different perspectives on the present and future threat of terrorism. Based on those readings, do you think that the likelihood of terrorism is real or overstated? Explain your answer.

2. Ehud Sprinzak argues that mass destruction terrorism does not pose a serious danger because terrorism "is not about killing." Do you agree with his analysis? Why or why not?

3. Matthew G. Devost, Brian K. Houghton, and Neil Allen Pollard contend that terrorists are becoming attracted to the use of technological tactics because information terrorism offers high visibility and low risk. In his interview with John Borland, William Church asserts that most terrorists have yet to adjust to the mindset needed to use information weapons and continue to prefer more physical methods, such as setting off bombs. Whose argument do you find more convincing and why?

Chapter 2

1. According to David C. Rapoport, democratic governments often inspire acts of violence. Do you think that the benefits (if any) of democracies outweigh the possibility of terrorism? Explain your answer.

2. Ehud Sprinzak and David Bar-Illan disagree over whether terrorists in Israel and the occupied territories are motivated by the actions of Israel or the Palestinian Authority. Whose argument do you find more convincing and why?

3. The viewpoints in this chapter deal in part with changes in modern society, such as urbanization and postwar politics, and their connection to terrorism. Which changes/events over the past century do you think have most strongly motivated terrorists? Explain your answer, drawing from the viewpoints and any related readings.

Chapter 3

1. ABC News conducted an interview with an alleged terrorist, Osama Bin Ladin. In that interview, Bin Ladin expressed a desire to kill Americans. Do you think that terrorists should be given the opportunity to justify their views or is it inappropriate publicity? Why or why not?

2. Martin Galvin, quoted extensively in Mark O'Connell's viewpoint, and the *Andersonstown News* disagree over whether bomb-

ings in Ireland can be justified. Under what circumstances, if any, do you think physical violence for political purposes can be validated? Explain your answer.

3. Martin Lindstedt argues that resistance to the U.S. government is justified because the government poses a threat to the freedom of its citizens. President Clinton contends that violence is not legitimate because Americans have broad freedoms and can address their grievances with the government through peaceful methods. Whose argument do you find more convincing and why?

CHAPTER 4

1. Robert W. Hahn asserts that airport security measures are ineffective because too few lives will be saved relative to the cost. Do you think that certain antiterrorism programs are too expensive or is any program that prevents deaths and injuries worth the expenditure? Explain your answer.

2. Holger Jensen contends that the United States needs to respond to international terrorism more aggressively. Raymond Close argues that America has a responsibility to settle international disputes without resorting to violence. Whose argument do you find more convincing? Why?

3. The authors in this chapter consider possible responses to terrorism. Which measures, if any, do you think would be most effective? Are there any other proposals you would suggest? Explain your answers.

ORGANIZATIONS TO CONTACT

The editors have compiled the following list of organizations concerned with the issues debated in this book. The descriptions are derived from materials provided by the organizations. All have publications or information available for interested readers. The list was compiled on the date of publication of the present volume; the information provided here may change. Be aware that many organizations take several weeks or longer to respond to inquiries, so allow as much time as possible.

American Civil Liberties Union (ACLU)
125 Broad St., 18th Fl., New York, NY 10004-2400
(212) 549-2500
e-mail: aclu@aclu.org • website: http://www.aclu.org
The American Civil Liberties Union is a national organization that works to defend Americans' civil rights guaranteed by the U.S. Constitution. It seeks to accomplish this goal through litigating, legislating, and educating the public on issues affecting individual freedom in the United States. In addition, the ACLU publishes and distributes policy statements, pamphlets, and press releases with titles such as "Government Designates 'Terrorist' Organizations" and "Most Americans Concerned About Losing Rights in Fight Against Terrorism."

Anti-Defamation League (ADL)
823 United Nations Plaza, New York, NY 10017
website: http://www.adl.org
The Anti-Defamation League's goal is to stop the defamation of the Jewish people and to secure justice and fair treatment to all people alike. The league has placed a spotlight on terrorism and has dedicated itself to alerting the government about the dangers of extremism. It offers many press releases on topics such as the background of Osama bin Laden and federal court action against local Hamas activists.

Cato Institute
1000 Massachusetts Ave. NW, Washington, DC 20001-5403
(202) 842-0200 • fax: (202) 842-3490
e-mail: cato@cato.org • website: http://www.cato.org
The Institute is a nonpartisan public policy research foundation dedicated to limiting the role of government and protecting individual liberties. It researches claims of discrimination and opposes affirmative action. The institute publishes the quarterly magazine *Regulation*, the bimonthly *Cato Policy Report*, and numerous policy papers with titles like "Combatting Terrorism, Protecting Freedom" and "Does U.S. Intervention Overseas Breed Terrorism?"

Chemical and Biological Arms Control Institute (CBACI)
2111 Eisenhower Ave., Suite 302, Alexandria, VA 22314
(703) 739-1538 • fax: (703) 739-1525
e-mail: cbaci@cbaci.org • website: http://www.cbaci.org

CBACI is a nonprofit corporation that promotes arms control and non-proliferation, with particular focus on the elimination of chemical and biological weapons. It fosters this goal by drawing on an extensive international network to provide an innovative program of research, analysis, technical support, and education. The institute publishes policy reports and monographs with titles that include "Combating NBC Terrorism: An Agenda for Enhancing International Cooperation" and "Deterrence and Chemical and Biological Weapons: Will It Work?"

Council on American-Islamic Relations (CAIR)
1050 17th St. NW, Suite 490, Washington, DC 20036
(202) 659-2247 • fax: (202) 659-2254
e-mail: cair1@ix.netcom.com • website: http://www.cair-net.org

CAIR is a nonprofit organization dedicated to presenting an Islamic perspective on public policy issues and to challenging the misrepresentations of Islam and Muslims. It fights discrimination against Muslims in America and lobbies political leaders on issues related to Islam and Muslims. Its publications include the quarterly newsletter *CAIR News* as well as periodic *Action Alerts*.

Federal Aviation Administration (FAA)
800 Independence Ave. SW, Washington, DC 20591
(800) 322-7873 • (202) 267-3484
website: http://www.faa.gov

The Federal Aviation Administration is the component of the U.S. Department of Transportation whose primary responsibility is the safety of civil aviation. The FAA's major functions include regulating civil aviation to promote safety and fulfill the requirements of national defense and encouraging the development of air commerce and civil aeronautics. Among its publications are *Technology Against Terrorism* and *Air Piracy, Airport Security, and International Terrorism: Winning the War Against Hijackers*.

Federal Bureau of Investigation (FBI)
935 Pennsylvania Ave. NW, Washington, DC 20535-0001
(202) 324-3000
website: http://www.fbi.gov

This is the official website of the FBI. It offers links to all topics relating to or handled by the FBI and, consequently, offers numerous articles on terrorism. Among the many titles are *The Threat to the United States Posed by Terrorists* and *FBI's Role in the Federal Response to the Use of Weapons of Mass Destruction*.

Heritage Foundation
214 Massachusetts Ave. NE, Washington, DC 20002-4999
(800) 544-4843 • (202) 546-4400 • fax: (202) 544-6979
e-mail: pubs@heritage.org • website: http://www.heritage.org

The foundation is a public policy research institute that advocates a strong national defense, limited government, and a free market system. It advocates the belief that the United States' primary role as a world leader is to eradicate the threat of terrorism. The foundation publishes the quarterly *Policy Review* as well as numerous articles on terrorism, including "The Changing Face of Middle Eastern Terrorism."

International Policy Institute for Counter-Terrorism (ICT)
PO Box 167, Herzlia 46150, Israel
972-9-9527277 • fax: 972-9-9513073
e-mail: mail@ict.org.il • website: http://www.ict.org.il

ICT is a research institute and think tank dedicated to developing public policy solutions to international terrorism. The institute applies an integrated solutions-oriented approach built on a foundation of real-world and practical experience. The ICT website is a comprehensive resource on international terrorism and counterterrorism, featuring an extensive database on terrorist organizations and attacks, an interactive forum, news updates, and articles on the motivations and methods of international terrorism. Selected publications include *Countering State-Sponsored Terrorism* and *Sleeping with the Enemy: Is Hamas Capable of Hudna?*

National Alliance
PO Box 90, Hillsboro, WV 24946
fax: (304) 653-4690
e-mail: national@natvan.com • website: http://www.natvan.com

The alliance believes in white superiority and advocates the creation of a white nation free of non-Aryan influence. It believes the increase in international terrorism is the result of U.S. political policies. It publishes the newsletter *Free Speech* and the magazine *National Vanguard*, both of which are offered on-line.

Washington Institute for Near East Policy
1828 L St. NW, Suite 1050, Washington, DC 20036
(202) 452-0650 • fax: (202) 223-5364
e-mail: info@washingtoninstitute.org
website: http://www.washingtoninstitute.org

The institute is an independent organization that produces research and analysis on the Middle East and U.S. policy in the region. It publishes numerous position papers and reports on Arab and Israeli politics and social developments, military affairs, and U.S. policy, including "Hamas: The Fundamentalist Challenge to the PLO," "Building for Peace: An American Strategy for the Middle East," and "Hezbollah's Vision of the West."

BIBLIOGRAPHY OF BOOKS

Richard Abanes — *American Militias: Rebellion, Racism, and Religion.* Downers Grove, IL: InterVarsity Press, 1996.

Tricia Andryszewski — *The Militia Movement in America: Before and After Oklahoma City.* Brookfield, CT: Millbrook Press, 1997.

Ron Arnold — *Ecoterror: The Violent Agenda to Save Nature.* Bellevue, WA: Free Enterprise Press, 1997.

Chip Berlet, ed. — *Eyes Right!: Challenging the Right Wing Backlash.* Boston: South End Press, 1995.

D.W. Brackett — *Holy Terror: Armageddon in Tokyo.* New York: Weatherhill, 1996.

Gavin Cameron — *Nuclear Terrorism: A Threat Assessment for the 21st Century.* New York: St. Martin's Press, 1999.

Richard J. Chasdi — *Serenade of Suffering: A Portrait of Middle East Terrorism, 1968–1993.* Lanham, MD: Lexington Books, 1999.

Cindy C. Combs — *Terrorism in the Twenty-First Century.* Upper Saddle River, NJ: Prentice Hall, 1997.

Martha Crenshaw, ed. — *Terrorism in Context.* Philadelphia: Pennsylvania State University Press, 1995.

Martha Crenshaw and John Pimlott, eds. — *Encyclopedia of World Terrorism.* Armonk, NY: Sharpe Reference, 1997.

Jim Cusack and Henry McDonald — *UVF.* Dublin, Ireland: Poolbeg, 1997.

Steven Emerson — *The Worldwide Jihad Movement: Militant Islam Targets the West.* Jerusalem, Israel: Institute of the World Jewish Congress, 1995.

Richard A. Falkenrath, Robert D. Newman, and Bradley A. Thayer — *America's Achilles' Heel: Nuclear, Biological, and Chemical Terrorism and Covert Attack.* Cambridge, MA: MIT Press, 1998.

David Hillel Gelernter — *Drawing Life: Surviving the Unabomber.* New York: Free Press, 1997.

John George and Laird Wilcox — *American Extremists: Militias, Supremacists, Klansmen, Communists, and Others.* Amherst, NY: Prometheus Books, 1996.

Adrian Guelke — *The Age of Terrorism and the International Political System.* London: Tauris, 1995.

Mark S. Hamm — *Apocalypse in Oklahoma: Waco and Ruby Ridge Revenged.* Boston: Northeastern University Press, 1997.

Philip B. Heymann	*Terrorism and America: A Commonsense Strategy for a Democratic Society.* Cambridge, MA: MIT Press, 1998.
Bruce Hoffman	*Inside Terrorism.* New York: Columbia University Press, 1998.
David Hoffman	*The Oklahoma City Bombing and the Politics of Terror.* Venice, CA: Feral House, 1998.
Jack Holland and Susan Phoenix	*Phoenix: Policing the Shadows.* London: Hodder & Stoughton, 1996.
Mark Huband	*Warriors of the Prophet: The Struggle for Islam.* Boulder, CO: Westview Press, 1998.
David E. Kaplan and Andrew Marshall	*The Cult at the End of the World: The Terrifying Story of the Aum Doomsday Cult, from the Subways of Tokyo to the Nuclear Arsenals of Russia.* New York: Crown, 1996.
Haig Khatchadourian	*The Morality of Terrorism.* New York: P. Lang, 1998.
Klanwatch Project of the Southern Poverty Law Center	*False Patriots: The Threat of Antigovernment Extremists.* Montgomery, AL: Southern Poverty Law Center, 1996.
Neil J. Kressel	*Mass Hate: The Global Rise of Genocide and Terror.* New York: Plenum Press, 1996.
Harvey W. Kushner	*Terrorism in America: A Structured Approach to Understanding the Terrorist Threat.* Springfield, IL: Charles C. Thomas, 1998.
Jaime Malamud-Goti	*Game Without End: State Terror and the Politics of Justice.* Norman: University of Oklahoma Press, 1996.
Louis R. Mizell	*Target U.S.A.: The Inside Story of the New Terrorist War.* New York: John Wiley and Sons, 1998.
Brigitte Nacos	*Terrorism and the Media: From the Iran Hostage Crisis to the Oklahoma City Bombing.* New York: Columbia University Press, 1996.
Kameel B. Nasr	*Arab and Israeli Terrorism: The Causes and Effects of Political Violence, 1936–1993.* Jefferson, NC: McFarland, 1997.
David Neiwert	*In God's Country: The Patriot Movement and the Pacific Northwest.* Pullman: Washington State University Press, 1999.
Benjamin Netanyahu	*Fighting Terrorism: How Democracies Can Defeat Domestic and International Terrorists.* New York: Farrar Straus Giroux, 1995.
James D. Nichols and Robert S. Papovich	*Freedom's End: Conspiracy in Oklahoma.* Decker, MI: Freedom's End, 1997.
Morgan Norval	*Triumph of Disorder: Islamic Fundamentalism, the New Face of War.* Bend, OR: Sligo Press, 1998.

Alan O'Day, ed. *Political Violence in Northern Ireland: Conflict and Conflict Resolution.* Westport, CT: Praeger, 1997.

Annamarie Oliverio *The State of Terror.* Albany: State University of New York Press, 1998.

Jim Ross and Paul Myers, eds. *We Will Never Forget: Eyewitness Accounts of the Bombing of the Oklahoma City Federal Building.* Austin, TX: Eakin Press, 1996.

Lyman Tower Sargent, ed. *Extremism in America: A Reader.* New York: New York University Press, 1995.

Glenn E. Schweitzer and Carole C. Dorsch *Superterrorism: Assassins, Mobsters, and Weapons of Mass Destruction.* New York: Plenum Press, 1998.

Donald M. Snow *Distant Thunder: Patterns of Conflict in the Developing World.* Armonk, NY: M.E. Sharpe, 1997.

Ehud Sprinzak *Brother Against Brother: Violence and Extremism in Israeli Politics from Altalena to the Rabin Assassination.* New York: Free Press, 1999.

Catherine McNicol Stock *Rural Radicals: Righteous Rage in the American Grain.* Ithaca, NY: Cornell University Press, 1996.

Raymond Tanter *Rogue Regimes: Terrorism and Proliferation.* New York: St. Martin's Press, 1998.

Joseba Zulaika and William A. Douglass *Terror and Taboo: The Follies, Fables, and Faces of Terrorism.* New York: Routledge, 1996.

INDEX

habeas corpus, 180–82
Habermas, Jurgen, 70
Haganah, 97
Haganah B, 97
Hahn, Robert W., 156
Halevi, Yossi Klein, 88
Hamami, Sheikh Jamil, 89
Hamas, 12, 60–61, 64, 65
  amateurism of, 21
  Arafat helps, 90
  does not oppose peace process, 88
  growth of, 85
  is dangerous, 142
  misrepresented view of, 84–85
  motivations of, for terrorism, 82–84, 85–86
  objectives of, 143–44
Hammond, Allen, 77
Hardman, Jacob, 68
Hatch, Orrin, 180–81
Hebrew University of Jerusalem, 48
Hezbollah, 12
hijackings, 33
Hizb'allah, 60–61
  reasons for terrorism by, 62–63
Hoffman, Bruce, 17, 60
Houghton, Brian K., 45
Hussein, king of Jordan, 82, 132
Hussein, Saddam, 43, 164, 170

Industrial Workers of the World, 74
information terrorism, 46–47
  vs. computer hackers, 54–55
  methods, 48–49
  military response to, 50
  no organized attempts of, 53
  as political crime, 47–48
  slow transition to, 52–53
  used by government, 53–54
Internal Revenue Service (IRS), 104
International Islamic Front for the Jihad Against Jews, 128
International Law Enforcement Academy, 178
Internet, 20, 36, 110
Internet Science Education Project, 52
intifada, 83
Iraq, 170
Irgun Svai Leumi, 97
Irish Northern Aid Committee, 117
Irish Republican Army (IRA), 13, 72
  actions are justified, 116–17
  information terrorism by, 52–53
Islam, 60
  demonization of, 171
is not a threat, 84
  moderate, 140
  terrorist groups from, 32–33
  see also jihad; Muslims
Islamic Jihad, 61, 83, 88
Islamic Resistance Movement, 135
Israel
  Arafat's charges against, 91
  and Ayash's death, 82
  establishment of, 136
  failure of, 141
  insults against Palestinians, 83–84
  response to terrorism, 164
  see also Jews

Jackson, Robert, 177
Japanese Red Army, 22
Jensen, Holger, 162
Jewish Kach, 65
Jews, 126
  domination of Muslim world by, 132–33
  relations with U.S., 128–29
  sale of land to, 134–35
jihad, 89, 133–34
  coordinating, 128
  defined, 139
  Muslim duty of, 136–37
  reasons for, 62–63
  on U.S./Jewish relations, 128–29
Johnson, Larry C., 26
Jordanian Islamic Action Front, 142
Jundallah, 64

Kaczynski, Theodore. See Unabomber
Kahane Chai, 12
Kenya, 14, 42, 80, 165
Khalas, Sikh Dal, 61
Khobar Towers, 164
Ku Klux Klan, 74
Kupperman, Robert, 46–47
Kurdish Workers Party (PKK), 27
Kyer, Gwynne, 32

La Belle disco, 28
law enforcement, 29–30
  counterterrorism, 177–78
  increased resources for, 29–30
Ledeen, Michael, 160
legislation. See Public Safety Act
Le Groupe Islamique Armé, 64
Levy, Gideon, 92
Lewinsky, Monica, 166
Libya, 29, 103
Lindstedt, Martin, 102

Lochamei Herut Israel, 97

Maine, Sir Henry, 74
Ma'moun, Hasan, 136
Marcuse, Herbert, 70
Marxist-Leninist groups, 33
Marzel, Baruch, 64
mass destruction weapons
  vs. conventional weapons, 44
  increase in, 36
  preoccupation with, 42–43
Matsumoto City incident, 37
McGuinness, Martin, 118
Middle Core organization, 22
Middle East
  peace process, threatened, 142
  Zionist domination, 132–33
  see also Islam; Israel; Muslims
Middle East Order, 132
military, U.S., 50
Mill, John Stuart, 76
Miller, John, 123
Miller, Judith, 43
minorities, 76
Montoneros, 95
Mosser, Thomas, 175
Moynihan, Daniel Patrick, 181
Munich Olympics, 29
Muslim Association, 85
Muslim Brotherhood, 85
Muslims
  Americans punished by, 125–26
  duty of jihad, 136–37
  fight for Allah, 126
  Jewish domination over, 132–33
  moderate, 140
  opposition to extremism, 141–42
  and sale of land to Jews, 135–36
  war with Somalia, 127
  see also Hamas; Hizb'allah; Islam; jihad

National Information Infrastructure
  (NII), 47–48
National Rifle Association (NRA), 180
nerve gas attacks, 22, 30, 37, 42–43,
  60, 110
  see also chemical weapons
Netanyahu, Binyamin, 82, 169
  on civil liberties, 177
  decisions against Palestinians, 84
Nida'ul Islam, 131
Noll, Mark A., 70
Non-Proliferation Treaty, 39
North Atlantic Treaty Organization
  (NATO), 126

Nunn, Sam, 35

O'Connell, Mark, 115
Oklahoma City bombing, 18, 28, 29,
  60, 110, 175
  as amateur terrorism, 20
  motivations for, 31–32
Omagh bombing, 116, 120
Omar, Sheik, 130
Oslo peace process, 85, 90
  Hamas does not oppose, 88
  Netanyahu does not believe in, 82

Paine, Thomas, 107–108
Pakistan, 128
Palestine Liberation Organization
  (PLO), 21, 132
  contrasted with Hamas, 85
  relations with Hamas, 88
Palestinian Intifada, 61
Palestinians, relations among, 88
  see also Hamas; Muslims
Pan Am Flight 73, 28
Pan Am Flight 103, 29, 31,154–55,
  165, 176–77, 178
paramilitary groups, 111
  see also terrorists
passenger-bag matching, 159
patriotism
  hating government is not, 112–13
Peace Press Association, 140
Pearson, Graham S., 43
People's Weekly Record, 13
Peres, Shimon, 82, 88, 143
Pickering, Thomas, 14
Pierce, William L., 106
Pollard, Neil Allen, 45
population growth, 78–79
prisons, 105–106
Public Safety Act
  is illiberal, 182–83
  origin of, 180–81
  weakens habeas corpus, 181–82
Pursuit of Loneliness, The (Slater), 70

Rabin, Yitzhak, 83, 92
Rahman, Sheik Omar Abdul, 130, 143
RAND–St. Andrews University
  Chronology of International
  Terrorism, 18
Ranstorp, Magnus, 59
Rapoport, David C., 73
Reagan, Ronald, 176
Real Irish Republican Army (RIRA)
  actions are justified, 116–17